YOUR INSTINCT

in Action

Also by T. D. Jakes

Reposition Yourself

Maximize the Moment

64 Lessons for a Life Without Limits

Making Great Decisions

The T. D. Jakes Relationship Bible

The Great Investment

The Ten Commandments of Working in a Hostile Environment

On the Seventh Day

Not Easily Broken

So You Call Yourself a Man?

Woman, Thou Art Loosed!

He-Motions

Mama Made the Difference

God's Leading Lady

Can You Stand to Be Blessed?

Let It Go: Forgive So You Can Be Forgiven

YOUR INSTINCT

in Action

—◆—

A Personal Application Guide
to *INSTINCT: The Power to Unleash
Your Inborn Drive*

T. D. JAKES

New York   Boston   Nashville

Unless otherwise indicated, Scripture quotations are taken from the King James Version of the Bible.

FaithWords

Hachette Book Group

237 Park Avenue

New York, NY 10017

www.faithwords.com

Printed in the United States of America

RRD-C

First Edition: September 2014

10 9 8 7 6 5 4 3 2 1

FaithWords is a division of Hachette Book Group, Inc.

The FaithWords name and logo are trademarks of Hachette Book Group, Inc.

The Hachette Speakers Bureau provides a wide range of authors for speaking events. To find out more, go to www.hachettespeakersbureau.com or call (866) 376-6591.

The publisher is not responsible for websites (or their content) that are not owned by the publisher.

ISBN: 978-1-4555-5887-2

Contents

Contents

A Letter from T. D. Jakes

Unleash Your Instincts!

Dear Friend,

I have never been more excited about a big idea than I am about following your instincts! While on safari in South Africa, I encountered a life-transforming moment as I sat between our two guides—one an expert PhD in zoology and the other a Zulu tribesman. The zoologist told me everything I could ever want to know about the many wild animals we encountered that day. However, the Zulu knew where to find them!

After a lifetime honing his instincts, the old Zulu took in all the data he so meticulously observed, from the scent on the wind to the width of broken branches near our trail, and processed it through his internal experience. There was no doubt he clearly trusted his instincts. While the zoologist was well educated about each animal's habits, the native tribesman received his education firsthand.

As I share in my book Instinct, *my concern is that in our twenty-first-century, technologically advanced culture, we move further and further away from trusting our natural inborn drive for success. We pursue diplomas and degrees, investigate internships and infrastructures, learn new software systems and social media skills, but we rarely get in touch with the God-given wisdom already residing within us.*

From my experience and observations, our true identity rarely enjoys the freedom to emerge without first enduring conformity, social modification, or outright suppression. Peer pressure, our family's expectations, and the demands of our circumstances all exert various amounts of force on who we really are. When we were younger, our instincts may have even guided us to hide parts of ourselves in order to keep them alive. We instinctively knew that we could not express our creativity, unleash our imagination, or announce our dreams without them being injured by the ridicule, rejection, or retaliation of others.

Now, however, you have the power to liberate yourself. You need no one else's permission to unleash the God-given essence of your identity! Whether you think you have the time, money, or other resources needed to uncover who you really are, it's vitally important that you discover your core and allow it to grow, develop, and flourish. This journey of self-discovery won't be easy, but if you have the courage to look within yourself and embrace all that you find there, your instincts can become a treasure map to your soul's satisfaction.

The clues are all around you if you're willing to look and listen. Your instincts can guide you to what you love but may not have allowed yourself to admit. They can help you recall the favorite memories of childhood and what gave you pleasure then. Was it building new, never-before-seen structures with Legos? Creating stories about your friends set on another planet? Caring for your pets with the love and attention of a new parent? Composing music on your phone app? Whatever once had the power to float your boat can still rock your world!

Nothing is off-limits as you explore the jungle of your own jurisdiction. You are the most fascinating person you will ever know! So don't cover up, deny, suppress, or pretend otherwise. Allow the true you to come out, the softer side, the edgier side, the creative side, the more organized side, the driven side, the liberated side, the "who cares what people think" side, and the "this makes me feel alive" side.

This is the soil in which you will discover seeds, planted long ago, waiting to burst through the surface of your consciousness and bear fruit. This is the galaxy of stars that can illuminate your journey through whatever darkness you may encounter. This is the area that can give you the satisfaction of knowing that you and you alone are doing what only you can do.

If this excavation process intrigues you, then I invite you to spend some time uncovering your greatest vital resources. I've created this guidebook to assist you in this process. Used as a companion to enhance and complement your reading of Instinct, *it will enable you to access your instincts, to discern how to use them, and to practice applying them in all areas of your life.*

We'll explore how you can become more self-aware of your instinctive gifts and when to supplement this awareness with information and education. Within these pages you will find exercises, tools, homework, and suggestions to ignite the tinder of talent already inside you. While these supplements are no substitute for the lifelong learning process, they can help you discern and utilize your greatest resource: your own instincts.

If you've wondered what you're missing, then now is the time to realize the answer—nothing! You already have all you need. It's simply a matter of going within and becoming acquainted with a vital part that's waiting to be exercised more fully. Once you grasp what's already within reach, then you can move mountains! Throughout this process, I will be here to coach, counsel, and cheer you on. Follow your instincts and you will discover the wild and wondrous territory—your most successful, dynamic future—blazing ahead!

*Instinctively excited and grateful
for all you're about to discover,
T. D. Jakes*

Chapter titles and numbers in this application guide correlate and refer to the same chapters in *Instinct: The Power to Unleash Your Inborn Drive*. You will find this guide most useful after reading the main book and then reviewing the relevant chapter; your understanding and experience of it will be enhanced as you complete this guide. The more willing you are to get deeply personal and in touch with your own life story, the more successful you will be in discovering the joy of living instinctively.

CHAPTER 1

Your Instinct Has a Rhythm

Now is the time to get in sync with your instinctive rhythm.

Your instincts have brought you to this time and place. It's no accident that you're reading *Instinct* right now and wanting to go deeper into its application and actualization in your own life. Something has been bubbling up within you for some time now. Call it dissatisfaction, an urge to explore, a restlessness with the status quo. You know it's time to make some positive changes and to become more of who you were meant to be. You know this instinctively.

Maybe you've read other books, attended seminars, enrolled in courses, and explored other options. Regardless of the insight these other items may have afforded, you remain at the edge of a breakthrough, eager to move from the margin to the main stage of your life. I'm convinced that your instincts already know what you need to do in order to make that move. My goal, through writing *Instinct* and this application guide, is to equip and empower you for this mining expedition of interior riches.

Yes, honing your instincts requires exploration and dedication, but your personal satisfaction will ignite your desires to achieve even greater dreams. You often expend time and energy in areas of advancement outside yourself without ever investing in what's inside you. Now is the time for you to uncover your greatest resources—yourself and your instincts—so that you can experience the life your heart longs to live.

God created men and women in his image and instilled his own divine impulse for creativity within each one. This internal compass, our instincts, can guide you beyond the trappings of success to the real treasure—the satisfaction of being and doing what you and you alone were created to be and to do.

Self quiz

On a scale of 1 to 10, with 1 being very far away and 10 being very near, rate how close you feel to living according to your best instincts.

1	2	3	4	5	6	7	8	9	10
Very Far Away				⟶				Very Near	

On a scale of 1 to 10, with 1 being very far away and 10 being very near, rate how close you feel to living the life you know you were created to live.

1	2	3	4	5	6	7	8	9	10
Very Far Away				⟶				Very Near	

Historically, _____ was the greatest obstacle to moving closer to the life I know I was created to live.

_____ is the largest barrier in my life right now to living the life I know I was created to live.

On a daily basis, I make gut decisions

☐ never to rarely

☐ once a day

☐ 2–3 times a day

☐ 4–6 times a day

☐ 7+ times a day

Based on my personal understanding of instinct before reading about it in the first chapter of *Instinct*, I defined it as:

_____

_____

Find Your Rhythm

You have only to look to cell biology to appreciate the vital importance of your inherent instincts. At the time of your conception, when the sperm and egg united and began forming your life, each cell had an identity with an intrinsic rhythm. Your cardio cells grew and united with other cardio cells, each cell vibrating with the rhythm that became your heartbeat. Aware of their purpose, these cells naturally attracted other cells within your body that were beating at the same pace.

If your very cells are imbued with instinctive wisdom from the Creator, then how much greater is the instinctive power instilled in you! The building blocks of your being function as a microcosm of what you're capable of achieving if you allow yourself to live instinctively.

When you allow your inner wisdom to filter your education, connect your experience, and compare your information, the resulting insight will allow you to discover the music of your life's symphony. And you will also find others with whom you share the same tempo—people who can share your dreams and stimulate you, collaborate with you, and cooperate with you to fulfill them. If you look around you, you shouldn't be surprised to realize that your instinctive journey is already in progress.

Introspective activity

Play a song that describes the external rhythm of your life presently. Keep in mind all the parts that contribute to the song: the tempo, the instruments, the melody, and the harmony, as well as the lyrics. Sit in a quiet place and listen to this piece of music as you consider the various ways it reflects your life at present.

Now play a song whose tempo reflects the natural rhythm within you. Similar to your thoughtful consideration of the "external" song, ask yourself how the individual parts of your "internal" selection reflects what's within you.

Pensive points

The song I played to represent the present external rhythm of my life is more like:

☐ a slow waltz

☐ a quickstep salsa

☐ improvisational jazz

☐ an acoustic guitar solo

☐ a wistful ballad

☐ a snappy pop tune

☐ a church hymn

☐ a country anthem

Other words I would use to describe this "external" song are:

_____   _____

_____   _____

The song I played to represent the natural rhythm within me is more like:

☐ a slow waltz

☐ a quickstep salsa

☐ improvisational jazz

☐ an acoustic guitar solo

☐ a wistful ballad

☐ a snappy pop tune

☐ a church hymn

☐ a country anthem

Choose ten words to describe your natural instinctive rhythm as precisely as possible.

_____   _____

_____   _____

	External rhythm of my life	*My natural rhythm*
Sounds like	_____	_____
Is slower	_____	_____
More evenly paced	_____	_____
Upbeat	_____	_____
Unpredictable	_____	_____

Journaling exercise

The steps I can take to bring the present external rhythm of my life into harmonious alignment with my natural rhythm are:

_____

_____

Reflection exercise

When I think about the people closest to me, friends and family, coworkers and colleagues, and others I see daily, these people seem to dance to my same rhythm, my same beat:

_____

_____

_____

Connect to Your Calling

If you haven't discovered your instinctive rhythm, you risk losing your connection to the natural tempo it provides for your life. You may feel uneasy and be aware that something's off-kilter or out or sorts. You may struggle in your relationships, stall in your career advancement, or sputter in your personal development. You watch others hit their stride and feel stuck, unable to find a way forward and uninterested in repeating the past. You're tempted to imitate their methods, but you're also aware that copying someone else's success is not what you're after.

There is a way forward, and your instincts already know what it is. Your instincts provide the key to your freedom. It may take several efforts to get the key to fit and the locks to turn, but you already instinctively know what you need to do. God has given you a greater purpose than just surviving day to day. Like a poorly fitting garment, your present reality cannot contain who you were meant to be. It's time to design something bigger and better, something that fits who you are and all that you were created to be. As Jesus teaches us, we should not put new wine in old wineskins (Matt. 9:14–17).

Scripture exercise

Read this New Testament passage from Matthew's Gospel (9:14–17) in at least two different versions. After comparing them, write the truth of these verses in your own words.

_____

_____

_____

If you want your life to be different, something has to change. You're already changing and will continue to evolve as long as you live. However, if you want to excel at your endeavors and enjoy the soul satisfaction that comes from your fulfilled purpose, then you must listen to your instincts. They know that the time is right for taking dramatic strides toward fulfilling your divine destiny, for realizing the potential that God has placed within you. The more in tune you become with your instinctive rhythm, the more you will enjoy the process of discovering your life's destination.

Visualization

Think back to when you felt the most contentment in your life.

Now list the variables that contributed to this season of satisfaction, the qualities that made it so satisfying.

_____   _____

_____   _____

_____   _____

Now think about where you are now.

List the variables that are satisfying and not satisfying.

Satisfying   *Not Satisfying*

_____   _____

_____   _____

_____   _____

Personal research exercise

Look through family photos of yourself as a child, paying close attention to casual and candid shots of you playing, performing, and participating in various activities.

List words that describe what the photos reveal about your true identity.

_____   _____

_____   _____

_____   _____

List childhood pursuits that still resonate with you today.

_____   _____

_____   _____

_____   _____

Journaling exercise

What longings do these memories stir, what dreams do they rekindle?

_____

_____

_____

_____

Research exercise

Choose one activity, hobby, or interest from childhood and search online for information about it. It could be anything from stargazing to collecting baseball cards, from quilting to gardening, from roller-skating to ballet dancing. You may even enjoy looking at children's books on this topic; they often cover basic information in ways that capture attention and inspire imagination.

Journaling exercise

Journal about your thoughts and feelings in response to your research. Include the childhood item of interest from above, perhaps by drawing it, pasting a picture from a magazine, or taping an online graphic you printed.

_____

_____

_____

_____

Practical exercise

Visit a craft store, sign up for a class, check out a book, or unpack collectible items related to your childhood hobby or special interest. Don't be afraid to approach this activity as a novice or beginner. You may discover that part of the fun in approaching this field of interest involves rekindling your childhood passion and curiosity.

"Never settle for less than God's best for your life"

(*Instinct*, p. 6).

CHAPTER 2

✦

Your Basic Instincts

*Your instincts provide wisdom
on how to survive as well as
how to thrive.*

Y our instincts have gotten you to where you are in life today. You've grown from being a baby into an adult because of your instinctive ability to survive, to adapt, to grow, and to learn. You were wired from birth to seek and find nourishment, to avoid pain, and to mature. You didn't have to learn how to breathe, how to eat, or how to avoid a hot fire. You've been equipped from birth with a basic survival mechanism to help you reach full maturation.

Even as an adult, your human body inherently seeks nourishment, protection, and comfort. "Fight or flight" remains a natural instinct that continues to guide you as you step back from the incoming car or defend yourself from someone who's intent on hurting you. God designed you to be resilient in body, mind, and soul even as if he elevated you above all the animals. Created in his image, you bear the imprint of his divinity, including a spiritual self that is eternal.

Scripture search

In the space provided, write out at least two Bible verses that reflect the fact that you're made in God's image. Choose two that remind you that your instincts are part of your divine DNA.

_____

_____

_____

As a result of being made in your Creator's image, you long for more than just food, water, shelter, and protection from danger. You long for meaning in your life, for a sense of fulfillment, purpose, and contentment. You believe you're here on this earth for a reason, and you remain restless until you discover it and live it. Your instincts instruct you not only on how to survive but also on how to thrive in this life. Just as your instincts can help you survive when physical needs go unmet, they can also help you fulfill your spiritual desire for meaning and joy.

Physical exercise

Observe an animal or insect following its natural instincts.

What intrigues me most about what I witnessed:

_____   _____

_____   _____

_____   _____

What similar survival instincts are in me (distinguish the items on your list from conditioning—such as eating at mealtimes):

_____   _____

_____   _____

_____   _____

Circle the most sharply tuned instinct on your list.

Meditation exercise

Think back to the last time your instincts prompted you to take action. What were the circumstances? How were your instincts functioning? Protecting you? Stretching you? Advancing your interests? Something else? Journal your memory and your thoughts about its significance.

_____

_____

Affirmation exercise

Write, say, or record an affirmation stating your spiritual longings for a meaningful life. Be sure to include ways you have tried to fulfill this longing and the results so far.

_____

_____

Your Instincts Evolve

Your instincts served you well as an infant and as a child, but as you developed your instincts became more sophisticated as well. They took in more information and data along with your experiences to use as a basis of comparison, a filter or lens to help you sort and sift thoughts, perceptions, feelings, and opportunities. However, chances are good that you also became conditioned to rely on your instincts less frequently and focus instead on your intellect, logic, empirical evidence, science, and technology.

Assaulted by a barrage of information and sensory stimulation each day, you're prone to lose touch with the voice inside you, the compelling wisdom that's often called a gut decision or hunch. Others in your life may discourage you from utilizing your instincts, insisting that they're too subjective, unsupported, or unscientific. "Stick to the facts," you're often told, all the while becoming less sensitive to the natural wisdom within yourself.

Other times you may listen to your instincts without acknowledging them as the source of your decision. Perhaps you chose to go with a gut feeling about taking one job over another. Maybe you're drawn to one career field or a certain specialty over all the others. Or consider the way certain people attract you with their ideas, charisma, and ability to inspire your dreams. You can't always explain your choices, but you're aware of times when you've simply gone with what seemed natural rather than a methodical analysis.

While many times your instincts prove accurate, there are certainly exceptions. You can't simply trust your subjective opinions on every decision. You need boundaries, reality checks, and objective data that put things in perspective. Like everyone, you have blind spots and you need help seeing what you can't see.

Over the course of your life, you've learned that listening to your instincts requires discernment and practice. You have to balance external intel with internal wisdom, allowing your instincts to synchronize and synthesize new associations, solutions, and relationships. Even if you're not living instinctively on a regular basis, you're likely aware of the power contained in this hidden resource within you.

Memory challenge

Remember the last time you allowed a gut instinct or hunch to guide your final decision and carefully recall the circumstances.

_____

_____

_____

_____

_____

Self-question series

- ☐ I felt like I was taking a big risk.
- ☐ I did not feel like I was taking a big risk.

Remember the last time you wished you'd listened to your instincts regarding a major decision.

- ☐ The consequences for not listening to my inner wisdom were good.
- ☐ I was aware of their reliability at the time.
- ☐ Afterward, I remained in touch with my instincts.
- ☐ Afterward, I distanced myself from my instincts.
- ☐ The consequences for not listening to my inner wisdom were bad.
- ☐ I was not aware of their unreliability at the time.
- ☐ Afterward, I remained in touch with my instincts.
- ☐ Afterward, I distanced myself from my instincts because of this inaccuracy.

Memory challenge

Recall a time when your instincts were not accurate. What message did you take away from this experience? What factors or variables may have contributed to your faulty instinctive impressions?

_____

_____

_____

You Just Know

Whether it's a sense that a new project is not what it appears or your impression that a new employee is a great investment, your instincts provide you with filtered information. You may or may not be aware of the experiences, observations, and incidents that go into your instinctive filter, but they are there. And often you may not be able to articulate how you know, but your confidence remains unshaken. Some things you just know!

And regardless of whether you realize it consciously or not, you know more about yourself than you realize. Because taken together, all the data—both objective and subjective—about who you are, what your unique talents are, and how to achieve their fulfillment you need is already in place. Whether you're young or old, married or divorced, employed or unemployed, you have distilled the essence of what you've learned about yourself and your life into your instincts.

Like a fine perfume, this instinctive essence can surprise you, inform you, and protect you if you'll let it. God wastes nothing, including your worst disappointments, most embarrassing failures, and costliest mistakes. He takes what you give him to fulfill the potential he instilled in you long ago.

Scripture search

Drawing on your favorite verses of Scripture as well as a concordance or an online search engine, list three Bible verses that reinforce this truth that God redeems everything in your life, including your failures.

_____

_____

_____

Each event, experience, and encounter in your life provides one more variable that ultimately strengthens your innate knowledge. With each new day, your instincts take in new data and recalibrate your awareness of how best to proceed. Your instincts operate like a highly sensitive compass, constantly picking up vibrations both big and small about your present location as well as the destination of your dreams.

The challenge, of course, is unpacking this stored wisdom and accessing it deliberately as you need it. A good place to start is identifying what you already know that you know: your preferences, your pet peeves, your personal likes and dislikes. This instinctive collection of distilled wisdom can then establish a foundation to which you return. It can steer you in directions to research what you don't know and fill in the gaps in your own instinctive knowledge. So with this in mind, let's think about what you know—and better yet, find ways to help you start acting on it today!

Instinctive wisdom exercise

The three most important instinctive truths I've learned about life so far. (Be as specific as possible to your own life—not just "Life is hard," but something like "I've learned life can be hard because of _____; however, I've also realized _____." Use one sentence for each truth.)

First Truth:_____

Second Truth:_____

Third Truth:_____

Now, what specific experiences, events, people, information, and observations have led you to each of these Three Truths?

Experiences:_____

Events:_____

People:_____

Information:_____

Observations:_____

Think through each one and jot down all the variables that come to mind. For instance, let's say your First Truth might be "I've learned that in order to achieve your dreams you need support from people who believe in you." Considering what's shaped this distilled truth, you might jot down things like "starting my own business, trying to go it alone right after I graduated, my best friend showing up for that awards ceremony, that time I spoke with our CEO."

Variables contributing to First Truth:

_____

_____

Variables contributing to Second Truth:

_____

_____

Variables contributing to Third Truth:

_____

_____

Finally, what have you learned about *yourself* in light of these Three Truths? How has each of these influenced a recent decision you've made? Have these Three Truths affected your life in more positive ways or more negative ways? How so?

_____

_____

Journaling exercise

Write a summary paragraph about what you know you know, including these Three Truths. Make it as current as possible, including the lessons you've instinctively learned most recently.

_____

_____

Practical exercise

Illustrate each of the these three instinctive distillations of wisdom with an appropriate symbol—a star, a compass, a tree, a mountain, or whatever occurs to you. Choose the symbol that most instinctively speaks to your heart's understanding of these truths. As long as the symbol resonates with you, it's a winner. There's no right or wrong choice. Use these symbols to create a reminder for yourself that you can see on a daily basis, such as on your mirror, your desk at work, or in your car.

"God, the master designer, has equipped us with a fundamental instinct that draws us to our divine purpose"

(*Instinct*, p. 16).

CHAPTER 3

◆

Your Instincts in Action

*Your success depends on your willingness
to act instinctively.*

You can learn so much about living instinctively by observing the habits of people who have sustained success for many years. These instinctively led individuals intrigue me, and I encourage you to become a lifelong student of observing how others have managed to overcome obstacles and to achieve their goals. While each may perform with excellence in different arenas, most people who sustain their success do so by honing their instincts and putting them into action.

You probably have certain people who instantly come to your mind. Instinctively successful individuals have not relied on others to define their roles or to determine their destinies. They have not followed anyone else's script but their own. They are not afraid to improvise, innovate, and insert themselves into risky situations that require creative solutions. They welcome change and view it as essential to their instinctively successful evolution.

Role model exercises

Who are the people you grew up admiring, both locally as well as on a national or an international level? What specifically did you admire about them? To what did you attribute their success?

PERSON	ADMIRED TRAIT	THEIR SUCCESS
_____	_____	_____
_____	_____	_____
_____	_____	_____

When have you tried to imitate the success of someone you admired? What were the results? What did you learn about yourself from this attempt? In what way did it sharpen your instincts for your own success?

PERSON	IMITATED TRAIT	OUTCOME
_____	_____	_____
_____	_____	_____
_____	_____	_____

Your Instinctive Evolution

In many ways, your parents and families of origin shaped your views on what it takes to be successful. Just as my parents wanted me and my siblings to know that there were worlds beyond the small community in West Virginia where we grew up, I'll bet your family also introduced you to various catalysts in order to whet your appetite for greater success in life. Your trips to the local library, the college football game, or the history museum may have planted seeds for your future instinctive evolution. You might not have even realized it at the time, but you received signals of future success throughout your upbringing. Whether these involved awards to win, material possessions to earn, status symbols to purchase, or exotic places to visit, these sparks kindled an instinctive fire of motivation within you.

When you follow your instincts, they will guide you toward more of what you long to know and to experience. And then they will take you beyond it all! How does this process work? While it varies from person to person, your instincts remain vigilant to your needs, wants, desires, and interests. Whether presidents or performers, movie stars or sports stars, most highly successful people have an insatiable curiosity about life—other people, other cultures, other ideas, other ways of doing things. They look for connections that others miss and use them to build bridges to their own dynamic futures. They aren't afraid to take risks, knowing they will gain information and insight even if they fail the first few times.

Paired exercise

If possible, complete the following and then compare answers with a parent, a sibling, or another trusted family member.

What message did you receive while growing up about what it took to be successful? What message did you receive about what it meant to follow your instincts? Did the two messages intersect in any way during your childhood and adolescence?

My family taught me _____ about being successful in life. These factors influenced their messages about success: _____, _____, and _____.

Memory challenge

List the plays, field trips, concerts, and cultural events that ignited your imagination when you were growing up. Did a particular performer stir something in your soul? A work of art beckon you to another world? A trip away from home open your eyes to a bigger world?

Plays:_____

Field trips:_____

Concerts:_____

Cultural events:_____

Other:_____

Visualization

Recall the most recent person, event, or opportunity that has ignited your imagination. When you visualize this situation, you see

_____

_____

_____

   This encounter rekindled _____ inside me. As a result, I instinctively reacted by _____.

Your Extra Edge

When your instincts lead you, they can elevate the mundane into the magical, transforming common ingredients into uncommon results. Your instincts operate as an internal innovator. They take what you put into them and create something bigger, brighter, and bolder.

As a kid, you probably practiced the art of using your imagination on a regular basis. The sandbox became the Sahara and the family dog became a camel as you transformed your surroundings through your creative vision. You didn't have to have actual props and visuals to create a scene, let alone a computer—you imagined it into being!

This imaginative muscle is the same one that gets exercised any time you face a problem for which you don't have an immediate solution. When old solutions no longer suffice, you know that you must create new ones. You have to see beyond the literal limitations, as well as through the emotional barriers, and envision a passage to the other side. When your options are limited and your resources depleted, then your instincts provide you with the extra edge you need to find a way forward.

Every adversity is the seed of an opportunity waiting to sprout. Instinctively successful people know not to take no for an answer. They push beyond the boundaries of barriers and persevere to new heights. When no other solutions present themselves, then it's time to create a new one. It's risky, it's hard work, it's demanding—and it's exhilarating! It's your instincts in action!

Role model exercise

List the people who continue to inspire you the most. Identify the traits that they seem to share. Now reflect on ways you see these same qualities in yourself.

_____

_____

Inspirational exercise

Write down your favorite works of art, music, theater, and literature that stir something deep within you. Look for themes or metaphors they may have in common and the ways they may be present in your life.

_____

_____

Application exercise

Choose one place or event that you've never visited or attended and make a date with yourself. Attend an opening at an art gallery, peruse the latest exhibit at the history museum, or take in a Broadway production. Explore the botanical gardens, the opera, the children's theater, a professional sporting event, or a pottery class. Choose whatever sparks your interest and make plans for your instinctive outing.

Journaling exercise

Describe your instinct-inspiring date with yourself. Note the details and moments that stand out to you as well as the aspects of your date that you enjoyed the most. Consider a follow-up adventure and make plans for another excursion.

_____

_____

"Trailblazing people move by instinct, because there is nothing outward that suggests that what they see inwardly is possible"

(_Instinct_, p. 25).

CHAPTER 4

◆

Where's Your Elephant?

*You don't have to go on safari
to find your elephant.*

Elephants, those big ideas, "aha! moments," and personal epiphanies that instinctively spur you to action, roam all around you. They often hide in plain sight in some of the most mundane details of your daily life. With your instincts to guide you, your elephants are never far away. The more you become aware of your instinctive compass, the more adept you become at locating those large, important discoveries in your own life.

Your instincts are the ultimate GPS device, always operating and assimilating new data, making new connections and comparing details from every moment of every day. Sometimes you may not hear the message your instincts are trying to tell you until after an experience. But sometimes you recognize your own instinctive wisdom in the midst of an event in ways that demand your attention. These revelations become the elephants of your instinctive imagination.

My South African safari was one such significant experience in my own life. Not only did the contrast between the zoologist guide and the Zulu tribesman remind me of the vital importance of instincts, but the encounter also became the impetus for an entire book and the life lessons on instinct I learned there. My instinct was to recognize the often underutilized power of instincts and to get the word out!

Your own experiences will reveal the same kind of powerful, life-changing messages if your instincts are attuned to them. You often become so chained to routine, to logic, to literal interpretations, that you miss the elephants all around you. Life is a constant teacher, and our instincts help tutor us in these timeless truths if we're willing to learn.

Sometimes a change of pace, place, or face helps you finally hear a message your instincts have been whispering for some time. When you travel, such as I did on my safari, you're forced to do things differently, to move to a new cultural rhythm, and to see things from various vantage points. These changes are often instrumental catalysts for your instinctive wisdom to emerge and to lead you to the elephants you're seeking.

Reflection exercises

What trip away from home has had the greatest impact on you? What were its major differences from what you were used to back at home? What were its major differences from what you expected?

_____

_____

_____

What recent experiences have led you to spot an elephant, a big idea that led you to make a change and to take action?

_____

_____

_____

Do you tend to rely on your "inner zoologist" or your "inner Zulu" more frequently? In other words, do you operate more on intellect or instinct in most situations? How can the two work in more harmonious alignment?

_____

_____

_____

_____

Your Own Instinctive Safari

Often you learn about something but fail to learn the heart of the thing itself. You can read all kinds of business models, company histories and mission statements, and quarterly reports—and of course you should in order to make informed decisions. But if you've never stepped inside the building, met its employees, or used its products, then you're lacking critical experience. Similarly, you can read dozens of great romance novels, watch lovers relate in the movies, and study the psychology of attraction. But if you never risk your heart to care for another person, then you know little about the actuality of love.

Like the zoologist, you can study animals online, in textbooks, under microscopes, and behind bars. But if you never live in their environment, watching them hunt, eat, mate, and die in the wilderness, then you miss the essence of knowing the animals firsthand. Sometimes you must step outside your usual methods of gathering information and experience the object of your study hands-on. You can't find your elephant if you're not in the bush!

Reflection exercises

What's an area in which you have relied on information rather than firsthand experience to make a decision? And vice versa: When have you relied on your experience instead of the available facts about a certain situation?

_____

_____

Name one area in which your instincts should be highly developed based on the amount of time you've invested in direct experience. Parenting? Banking? Sales? Home repairs? Writing? Teaching? Baking? Cleaning? Talking? What are the "elephants" your instinctive expertise has helped you find?

_____

_____

Self quiz

Consider the following scenario: You've just taken a new job in a city hundreds of miles away from your present home. You will need to find a new home for you and your family as soon as possible. Which of the following three people would you most want to talk with about your impending move? List your reason for choosing each of your three below your selections.

☐ a top real estate agent in your new locale

☐ your boss at the new job

☐ a coworker with kids the same age as yours who moved there three years ago

☐ a pastor at a large, popular church in your new city

☐ a retired teacher who has lived her entire life in your new city

☐ an old friend from high school who now lives near your new office

☐ a construction foreman for a leading home builder in your new city

☐ a restaurant owner in the neighborhood you like best in the new city

Your choices likely reflect your priorities for your new home. If your kids and their education are a priority, you naturally would want to talk with other parents, teachers, and educators. If you're interested in making an investment in your home purchase, then you would seek the input of builders and Realtors in the area. You would want to look at the numbers, the facts, and the data about your move, but you would also want some firsthand impressions and discussion with people who know the area as well as my Zulu tribesman knew the bush.

Assessment exercise

With this sense of focusing on your present priorities, what did you learn about what's most important to you right now? How have your instincts confirmed these priorities in other ways?

_____

_____

Your Guide Inside

If you want to find the "elephant" you're seeking in your own life, then you must follow your instincts and not just your intellect. You certainly want as many facts as possible about any endeavor you're about to attempt. There's never an excuse for not doing due diligence unless there's absolutely no time for it. However, even when you have all the available information spread about before you, there's still something missing.

Each of us sees the world differently. If you've ever been involved in a fender bender and talked to witnesses, then you know that each one likely saw the accident a different way. Similarly, relationships, board meetings, and classroom interactions can seem one way to one party and yet be read—or misread—entirely differently by others in attendance. While this makes communication and collaboration challenging at times, it also reinforces the priceless gift contained in each person's unique perspective.

Why do you see the same event, person, or meeting differently than other people? Because you're filtering it through what you already know, what you want to know, and what you expect to find out. Sometimes you have to pay closer attention in order to sharpen your instincts. If you're missing details because you didn't observe accurately, then you cannot expect your instincts to be on target. If you're ignoring factual information, then your instincts will not be as strong as if you have all the pieces.

The key to harnessing your instincts into action is examining the variables that go into your instinctive fuel tank. Certain experiences may bias you with no good reason except for a onetime encounter. Other preferences may not be pertinent to the decision at hand; you may love brown eyes, but they should not affect your choice of doctor.

You have to take your lenses apart and consider each one separately, noting how each one colors what you take in individually as well as in conjunction with the other lenses. If you want to know where to find the elephant with the same acutely keen instincts as the Zulu tribesman I encountered, then you must be willing to explore the depths of your own heart.

Goal setting exercise

_____ is the "elephant" I'm currently seeking in my life. My pursuit of this goal, big idea, or revelation has already taught me:

_____

_____

If I had more _____, I would be able to find my elephant.

Talking to _____ about my elephant hunt would be helpful to my search.

Once I discover my elephant, I expect _____ to happen.

One action I can take today in pursuit of my elephant is

_____

_____

Pensive points

As we've seen, our instincts combine a variety of external and internal variables to create a filter for how we take in information, assess it, and reach decisions. All of the following variables contribute to most people's instincts. As you think through your specific responses, also consider which of these variables you rely on most frequently.

What are the *key losses* in your life that influence your instincts?

_____

_____

_____

What are the *big achievements* in your life that affect your instincts?

_____

_____

_____

YOUR INSTINCT IN ACTION

What *personal biases* involving other people likely undermine the accuracy of your instincts? What's the basis for these biases?

_____

_____

_____

What *areas of special interest* currently inform your instincts?

_____

_____

_____

What *future expectations* contribute to your instincts?

_____

_____

_____

What *past wounds* shape the accuracy of your instincts?

_____

_____

_____

Practical exercise

What *present action* can you take today to improve your instincts' reliability? Describe one habit that if practiced regularly, could help you sharpen and hone your instincts. For example, maybe you need to visit your company's production department on a weekly basis in order to feed your curiosity about product design. Or maybe it's simply reading monthly journals about a passionate topic or field of interest.

_____

_____

_____

"Living by instinct elevates your ability to know where you're going and how to get there. It can help you know when to slow down and step back and when to accelerate and step up"

(*Instinct*, p. 44).

CHAPTER 5

Your Instinct or You're Extinct

*Your instincts can help you crack
the code to your uniqueness.*

With your instincts, as with many aspects of life, you often get what you expect to get. As a kid, you may have never tried broccoli and just assumed that you hated its taste. However, as an adult you finally realize that your conclusion (you hate broccoli) is in error because it lacks supporting evidence (since you've never tried it). So you finally taste broccoli and hold on to your bias, in turn creating a self-fulfilling prophecy. "Yep, I was right," you say to yourself, "that green stuff does indeed taste nasty!"

On the other hand, if you taste broccoli with an open mind (and a little cheese sauce!), then you discover that you've been missing out on something delicious. You then realize that your assumptions and preferences change just as your body, mind, and emotions change over time. You don't want to taint your instincts with information that's no longer true, if in fact it ever was. You must learn to adapt your instincts, releasing old data or unsupported conclusions so that your instinctive compass can operate more accurately.

You can't rely on your instincts exclusively (especially when they're based on old or biased information) and expect them to be accurate and reliable every time. Similarly, you cannot ignore them and base decisions solely on facts and figures. The solution is to balance one with the other, allowing data to inform your instincts and your instincts to read between the lines of the data. If you're going to sharpen your instincts into a viable tool for actualizing your dreams, then you must be willing to keep them tethered to objective, factual, and up-to-date information. When factual knowledge and instinctive wisdom work in tandem, you will grow by leaps and bounds!

Self-assessment exercise

Do you consider yourself more of a logical, rational kind of person or more of an emotional, experiential type? More of a left-brain individual who prefers linear, sequential information? Or more of a right-brain, creative individual who assimilates information more by associative patterns?

_____

_____

_____

Memory challenge

Think of a time in the past when you contributed to a self-fulfilling prophecy by settling for what you expected to get. How did your perceptions of the situation prevent you from seeing matters more objectively? How did your perceptions in turn impact your instincts' accuracy?

_____

_____

_____

When have you made a balanced decision based on a combination of instinct and information? What were the results? What prevents you from taking a more balanced approach with most of your decisions?

_____

_____

_____

Your Instinctive Identity

When you were growing up, perhaps especially when you were a teenager, you likely experimented with a variety of styles, preferences, and personalities on your journey to discover your authentic self. You might have tried various kinds of clothing, music, and self-expression until you found the ones that seemed natural. It might have been a frustrating process of trial and error that left you wondering how all the pieces fit together. Maybe you liked classical music but trendy fashions, retro décor but the latest tech gadgets. It's unusual to find one style or lifestyle that fits you comprehensively.

This explains why borrowing a little from many different styles allows you to create your own unique sensibility. As long as you're committed to finding your true uniqueness, then imitation has a place in the process of developing and honing your instincts. When you're merely trying on the garments of another person's styles, successes, and selections, you can discover what truly fits.

Visualization

Imagine sitting at a table in your favorite restaurant. As the lunch crowds disperse, you look over at the table across from you and see someone who appears to be your identical twin in almost every way. What do you see as you scrutinize this person? What is she wearing? What is he doing? What characteristics would you use to describe someone who's your twin?

Memory challenge

How did you try to find yourself during your childhood and adolescence? What sports did you play? Musical instruments? What other extracurricular activities did you explore? Which interests took root as a kind of natural fit or personal passion, and which ones faded away as you learned more about yourself?

How would you describe your personal style when you were a teenager? Punk? Goth? Preppy? Jock? Geek chic? Designer diva? *GQ* gangsta? Something all your own? What fads or trends did you experiment with? Which ones seemed like a true reflection of who you are? What evidence of your fashion experimentation remains in your present style sensibilities?

Instinctive influence exercise

What catches your eye as you scroll through your e-mail or surf online? Which ones do you read and bookmark, and which do you skip and delete?

_____

_____

_____

Who are the people in the public eye who intrigue and inspire you by their personality, talent, and sense of style? Whose life story resonates with your own as you aspire to greater achievements in your own life?

_____

_____

_____

Decode Your Design

It's never too late to unpack more of the treasure stored within you. And asking yourself questions and paying attention to what makes your heart beat faster are two of the best ways of opening this instinctive treasure chest. I've encouraged you to reminisce about your childhood as well as to reflect on some of your teenage excursions into identity. But what about where you are now?

Affirmation

What are the threads, the through lines of continuity and consistency, interwoven throughout your entire life? What is their pattern, the divine design that signals something greater than what you've yet accomplished? Write your response as a statement of affirmation, one to which you can return when you face self-doubt or uncertainty.

_____

_____

Sometimes you need help even as you delve deeper into your own internal wisdom. The feedback of others, the results of past endeavors, and your own comments from past events can all provide priceless revelations that stimulate your instincts. Once you recognize these patterns, preferences, and proclivities, you can begin looking for larger patterns and new associations. Never forget for one moment how fascinating you really are!

Research exercise

Look through past performance evaluations at work, client reports, and project assessments. Review articles you've written, research papers for classes, and journal entries (if you've kept a journal). Use an online search engine such as Google to see what the rest of the world discovers when they type in your name. What major clues to your identity stand out to you? What surprises you the most as you consider these past pieces of evidence?

_____

_____

Interactive exercise

Many managers and executives often take part in "360-degree" evaluations in which numerous colleagues, coworkers, clients, and associates complete an assessment and sometimes an interview regarding the subject. It's thought that seeing oneself through the eyes of major stakeholders in your career can illuminate your strengths, weaknesses, and blind spots. Conduct your own 360-degree assessment by asking key people from each of the following areas to provide written and verbal feedback on what they know and believe about the kind of person you are.

☐ Family Area (such as a spouse, a sibling, an adult child, or a parent)

☐ Personal Area (such as a close friend or confidant)

☐ Career Area (such as a coworker, colleague, or supervisor)

☐ Community Area (such as a pastor, volunteer coordinator, or community leader who knows you well)

Here are some questions you might ask:

☐ What interpersonal skills do I demonstrate?

☐ How could I improve my interpersonal skills?

☐ What interpersonal skills should I work on developing?

☐ How am I as a relationship builder?

☐ How could I improve my relationship skills?

☐ Do I effectively solve problems?

☐ If so, what are my best skills in solving problems?

☐ Where do I need work to improve my problem-solving skills?

☐ Do I seem motivated?

☐ In what ways? In what ways not?

☐ Honestly tell me a situation where you experienced difficulty with me.

☐ Do you feel I am accomplishing more, becoming more effective, and continuously improving?

☐ What would you recommend I do to improve?

☐ Do I make thorough plans and follow through?

☐ What would you recommend I do to improve?

☐ Do I pay attention to details you feel are important?

☐ What would you recommend I do to improve?

☐ Do I prioritize and follow through on the priorities I set?

☐ Are my priorities appropriate in your view?

☐ What would you recommend I do to improve?

☐ How well do you feel I manage my time?

☐ Am I consistently late? Do I keep you waiting?

☐ Do I exhibit leadership? If so, please provide examples.

☐ If not, how could I improve my leadership?

☐ Am I a good team player?

☐ In what ways? In what ways not?

☐ Do I put the success of the team before my own needs?

☐ In what ways? In what ways not?

☐ Do you feel you can usually depend on me to keep my commitments?

☐ Give me an example of a time when I was dependable and one when I dropped the ball.

Turn to the Appendix at the end of this workbook and take the "Instinctive Animal Evaluation" questionnaire. Although it's not scientific, you may have some fun discovering your own law of the jungle!

Evaluation exercise

After you take the "Instinctive Animal Evaluation" questionnaire, consider the result. Did you turn out to be the animal you thought you would be? Which animal would you choose to be regardless of how you scored? Why do you find this animal appealing?

_____

_____

_____

"If you live instinctively, these critics will never impede your progress for more than a few moments. In my own life, I've never had a hater who's doing better than me!"

(*Instinct*, p. 54).

CHAPTER 6

❖

Your Instinctive Sense of Direction

*Your instincts provide you with the
resourceful resilience needed to succeed.*

When you go through trials, adversity, and disappointments, your instincts can help you find the strength to persevere by utilizing your remaining resources. My life has been filled with numerous obstacles and barriers, but at each turn I've refused to let them impede my progress toward something greater. You may not realize just how resourceful you've been throughout your life until you pause to consider how far you've come.

Memory challenge

Look back over your life and identify three obstacles you've overcome to get where you are now. How did you get through those barriers? What actions did you take in order to keep moving toward your goals? Who supported or encouraged you during these times?

_____

_____

While you may not be pursuing your primary passion at present, you can know without a doubt that where you are right now is a stepping-stone on your journey. Even when your life takes unexpected detours and encounters temporary road-blocks, your instincts will still guide you like a divine GPS system. You may feel as if you're having to defer your dreams in order to pay the bills, take care of your family, or manage your responsibilities. However, during these trials you must keep the faith and understand that what you're going through is part of the process toward your instinctive success.

In light of your life's passionate destination, your present path may not seem logical, rational, or strategic. But even when your choices are borne of necessity and desperation, you must realize that these are incredible catalysts for sending your instincts into overdrive. If you let them, your instincts can guide you through the worst storms and allow you to find safe passage until the next safe harbor.

Pensive points

When have you faced a trial or season of adversity and been forced to come up with a survival solution? How did your instincts play a role in moving through this obstacle?

_____

_____

What prevents you from trusting your instincts when confronted with a problem, conflict, or disappointment in your life?

_____

_____

What fears or concerns about your future currently prevent you from trusting your instincts more fully?

_____

_____

Where You're Going

One of the key resources you have when faced with adversity is your team of supporting players. As I've shared many times, throughout my life I've felt a keen sense of responsibility to provide for my family regardless of the sacrifice involved. Similarly, I feel a sense of loyalty with my employees and want to honor their trust in me by leading our team successfully.

But these relationships work in both directions. I cannot imagine how I would have been able to trust my instincts and take instinctive actions throughout my life without the emotional and spiritual support of my wife and family, my pastoral team and church members, and my colleagues and business associates. You need others who believe in you and affirm your instincts, not people who constantly second-guess and plant seeds of doubt. There's a place for being questioned and challenged and held accountable for your instinctive decisions, but a bond of trust must be firmly established before it can be tested.

Relationship assessment exercise

Who are the key people in your life who have consistently supported you in your instinctive endeavors? Write down their names in the categories below.

☐ Family:

☐ Friends:

☐ Colleagues and Coworkers:

☐ Teachers and Mentors:

☐ Church Family and Spiritual Leaders:

☐ Others:

Who are the people who have caused you to doubt yourself and to ignore your instincts? What role do they currently play in your life? How can you disconnect their influence from your present and future endeavors?

_____

_____

Who are the people you would currently like to see become more involved with your goals and aspirations? How can they help you take instinctive action to further your dreams?

_____

_____

Keep Your Thrill Alive

While you probably do not need additional fears to fight, you do need the ongoing stimulation of a healthy challenge. Once you master an area or become familiar with your responsibilities, all too often you become complacent. You become inclined to settle for satisfactory instead of true satisfaction. You allow your routines to numb your instinctive sensibilities and step back from the risks needed to break out of the rut.

If you want to excel at living instinctively, then you must constantly challenge yourself in positive, dream-affirming, talent-stretching ways. You must surround yourself with other positive, progressive, instinctively attuned individuals who will stimulate, inspire, and motivate you to your full potential. On the other hand, you must remove yourself from relationships—whether personal or professional—that seek to diminish your dreams and discount your directives.

You need people in your life who are in touch with their instincts and model instinctive living and risk taking. Trust as well as mutual respect is essential. When you encounter these kinds of people, you're able to sharpen one another's instincts and move forward in progressive ways that are dynamic, innovative, and exhilarating!

Practical exercise

Make a list of the people currently in your life who see your true talents and potential and challenge you accordingly. Choose at least one to invite to lunch as a thank-you for their belief, support, and encouragement.

_____

_____

Memory challenge

Describe a time when you've experienced a "scare me again" kind of moment, as described on pages 65–66 of *Instinct*. What was the challenge you faced? In what ways did it terrify you? Excite you? Inspire you? What role did your instincts play in going through this experience?

_____

_____

Role model exercise

List three to five successful people in your community, individuals who clearly take risks and seem comfortable following their instincts. Choose one you can ask to mentor you, then e-mail or call this person to arrange a meeting. If he or she is unavailable as a mentor, choose another person on your list until you have an "instinctive mentor" with whom you can meet at least once a month.

_____

_____

"I'm convinced the only way you can develop your true gifts, your creative instincts, is by embracing a vision so daunting that your heart goes running up the steps like a child, screaming with delight because you have a challenge that equals your creativity"

(*Instinct*, p. 66).

CHAPTER 7

❖

Your Instincts Turned Inside Out

When you live instinctively, your mistakes become your milestones.

As you learn to live instinctively, you must never be afraid of failing, only of failing to try. Sometimes our most painful, glaring mistakes can become the instinctive turning points of transformation. When you take a risk, create an experiment, or test a hypothesis, you often discover something unexpected, unpredictable, and unprecedented. These discoveries have led many inventors and innovators to revelations, epiphanies, and products that they would never have had if they had not failed and kept trying.

If you can suspend judging and condemning yourself for your failures, then you can engage with the lessons to be learned from them. If you can ignore the criticisms and derisive comments from others, then you can absorb an instinctive awareness of what to do differently next time. Your instincts constantly monitor all that you're doing, thinking, saying, and risking, looking for insight to guide you to new heights.

Creative individuals know that they have to give themselves permission to play, to discover, to attempt, and—yes—to fail in order to unleash their talent.

Painters have to make sketches of things that never end up in their paintings. Composers must endure the disharmony of discordant notes before the right combination flows together. Writers must continually draft and revise and revise some more in order to express their ideas and stories.

If creative people gave up the first time their art didn't come together, then we would have nothing but empty museums, libraries, and concert halls! Our instincts can transform our greatest trials into our most surprising triumphs if we follow their wisdom and persevere in our attempts. Like the legendary alchemists, our instincts turn lead into gold.

Reflective exercise

In what areas of your life have you failed repeatedly? What has emerged from your efforts and attempts? How have you handled these failures in your life? What have you learned from them that has influenced your instincts?

_____

_____

_____

Describe the inner voice that typically criticizes your actions and condemns your intentions. If you don't have one, then count your blessings, because most of us do! Who has contributed to the formation of your inner critic? Parents? Partners? Teachers? Bosses? Others?

_____

_____

_____

Affirmation

What would you instinctively like to say in response to your inner critic? What risks would you take if you knew that no one—not even yourself—would criticize your actions? Write your response as a self-affirming statement of confident assertion in your own abilities to succeed by following your instincts.

_____

_____

_____

_____

Your Instinct Adapts

When faced with seemingly insurmountable adversity and hardship, your instincts enable you to adapt in order to survive. Conditions and circumstances that you could never imagine yourself enduring and surviving somehow become manageable when you allow your instincts to lead you moment by moment and day by day.

Survivors of war, slavery, brutal crimes, and natural disasters somehow find the strength and resiliency to keep going. It's devastatingly difficult and in some cases impossible to fathom. Yet the human spirit, guided by divinely designed instincts, cannot be vanquished.

In many cases, you not only survive but also discover new dimensions to your personality. When confronted with life-threatening dangers, you often summon reserves of strength previously undetected. With your back against the wall, you surprise yourself with new levels of courage and creativity.

Reflective exercise

When have your instincts helped you adapt to new changes? What prior expectations and assumptions did you have to release in order to accept these changes? Why?

_____

_____

How have your instincts enabled you to survive difficult circumstances? What wisdom about yourself emerged as you endured this painful season? What new abilities, talents, and gifts did you discover within yourself?

_____

_____

What are the greatest challenges you've overcome in your life? How have they influenced the person you are today? How have they strengthened your instinct for survival?

_____

_____

Your Instinct Inspires

While you might be tempted to think only artists and writers need inspiration, you too rely on your imagination for ideas every day. If one route to work is blocked, you take another. If you can't convince a client to meet at your office, you go to hers. If a big project goes off the tracks, you look for ways to restore its successful trajectory. One outfit doesn't look good, so you put together one that looks beautiful.

Your instincts will guide you beyond familiar paths and predictable solutions if you're willing to follow them outside the box. Too often, you settle for what's been done before the way it's been done before. You limit yourself without even realizing it. With your instincts as your muse, you can discover new patterns, brilliant systems, and amazing conceptual relationships that shake up the status quo.

Sometimes your most inspired solutions emerge from the unlikeliest places. You must remember that your instincts absorb inspiration from every direction, especially the ones that tend to surprise you the most. Like Nike's Bill Bowerman creating a tennis shoe tread after glimpsing a waffle iron, you can make inspired associations that astound you with their practicality and functionality. Your instincts function as creative catalysts for your ultimate success. You need only to pay attention and to take action.

Self-assessment exercise

When faced with a new project, product, or problem, how do you usually begin the process of tackling it? Do you have a system or do you approach each new initiative differently? What methods or systems have worked most successfully for you in past endeavors? Did you usually work more productively by yourself or as part of a team?

_____

_____

Inspirational exercise

Make a list of anything that is currently inspiring you. These items may be photographs, articles, books, blogs, websites, paintings, sculpture, cars, interior designs, specific pieces of clothing, particular designers—anything that's appealing to you, stirring something inside you, and igniting ideas of your own.

_____

_____

Flip through a stack of magazines and focus only on visual images. Cut out any picture, graphic, image, scene, or artwork that evokes something in you. You don't have to love it—in fact, you may even hate it!—but it definitely triggers strong emotions.

_____

_____

Sort through the items you clipped and choose five to place in a spot where you can see them for the next week. On the back of or below each one, jot down why you find it so evocative, intriguing, or emotionally charged.

Practical exercise

Visit an unusual place that you would not normally encounter but have always been curious about. It may be the local florist's shop, an animal shelter, the history museum, or a local tourist attraction.

"Our instincts inspire us to look beyond the usual and identify the unusual. If we're attuned, our instincts transfer principles from one field of study to another, mix metaphors that yield new insights, and create fresh designs from tired traditions"

(*Instinct*, p. 77).

CHAPTER 8

✦

Your Instincts to Increase

*Your instincts will lead you to create
and to increase.*

There's nothing wrong with wanting more than you have. In fact, it's probably part of the divine impulse compelling you to live out God's instruction to Adam and Eve: "Be fruitful and multiply" (Gen. 1:28). Perhaps you assumed this divine command referred only to procreation, but I'm convinced that the kind of creation God has in mind involves more than just conceiving children.

Scriptural exercise

Read Genesis 1 in your favorite version of the Bible. Do you agree that God wants men and women to create more than just children? Why or why not? Indicate details within the account of Creation to support your viewpoint.

_____

_____

As you consider the implications of being created in God's image, recognize this important distinction regarding your divine purpose. You are made to create as an active agent of the divine. You are not made to live passively as a dependent on the creativity of others. This contrast is crucial to your ability to achieve instinctive success. If your primary motivation is just to consume and to enjoy immediate gratification, then you will live an unhappy life. You are made for much more than being a consumer. You are made to create a divine legacy unique to yourself.

In order to live instinctively, you must keep your divine creative purpose in mind. You must be willing to be honest with yourself, look within your heart and motives, and identify greed. It's an ugly word, and not one you probably like applying to yourself. But you must learn to distinguish the negative inclination to consume in order to fill a void in your life versus the positive instinct to create on a larger and larger scale.

Greed seeks to give you a false sense of happiness through material possessions and accumulated wealth. The instinct to increase, on the other hand, guides you to your most creative, productive arenas, the destination of your dreams, where you can live out of your instinctive purpose. When greed motivates you, there's never enough—not enough money, not enough stuff, and not enough time to enjoy any of it. When the instinct to increase motivates you, there's more than enough, and it's continually multiplying!

Success breeds success. When you allow your instincts to guide you and achieve success in one area, you will soon discover that more doors will open. Your ability to navigate your ascension in one field transfers to increased opportunities in other fields. The financial and material success will likely follow, but it's secondary to the innate personal satisfaction that emerges when you're living out your instinctive and divinely appointed purpose.

Reflective exercise

Have you experienced times when you struggled with your success? Ever felt unworthy or even guilty for enjoying your accomplishments? What contributes to this struggle?

_____

_____

Have you ever considered yourself greedy or too ambitious? Have others made you feel like you didn't deserve the advancements you worked hard to achieve?

_____

_____

When have you experienced the instinct to increase? How has success in one area of your life planted seeds for success in other areas? How can you tell the difference between greed and instinctive fruitfulness?

_____

_____

Leaving Your Cages

One of the greatest barriers to your advancement is your current comfort zone. Even if you're dissatisfied and disappointed with your present circumstances, at least they seem familiar and predictable. Rather than having to take risks and venture out into freedom, you may be tempted to settle for the back corner of the cage where you attempt to tell yourself you're satisfied. Or you might tell yourself that your cage provides everything you need, that it's a safer place than the risky wilderness beckoning your instincts from beyond your confinement.

But something keeps drawing you back to the door, to your vision beyond the bars of your cage. Like the lion confined in his pen at the zoo, you instinctively long to experience greater freedom and a larger adventure than your cell permits. This yearning is universal; however, the timing, pace, and particular destination beyond your cage is unique. No one can tell you the right time to leave your cage of conformity, and no one can do it for you.

It's simply the magnetic attraction you have for something beyond where you find yourself. You may not know exactly what it is or what you'll find, but you know that you have to explore opportunities or live with regret the rest of your life. But you don't have to live with that regret. If you're willing to follow your instincts, you will discover an entire world beyond the confines of your current cage!

Self-assessment exercise

How would you describe your present circumstances? In what areas of your life are you presently most satisfied and comfortable? Which areas feel more unsettled and restless?

_____

_____

What do you fear most about taking the risk to step out of your current cage? What would you risk losing? What could you potentially gain?

_____

_____

When have you ventured out of your comfortable cage in the past? Which risks have allowed you to progress and experience a bigger world beyond where you began?

_____

_____

Your Instinct to Leap

While caution and moderation are important virtues, they must be tempered by risk and decisiveness. When opportunity knocks, you must be prepared to answer the door rather than bury your head under the covers and pretend to sleep. Your instincts provide you with the sense of timing, selection, and action that allows you to take big leaps of faith.

Sometimes you may experience a plateau, especially after attaining what you thought you wanted. You get the corner office, have the beautiful home, delight in your healthy family, and earn more than enough to pay the bills. You worked so hard to arrive at this place, and yet something's still missing. It's not quite what you thought it was, after all. Or maybe it's exactly what you wanted, but now your interests have shifted.

When you peel away the layers of conditioning, living for others, and conforming to societal expectations, you discover that instinctive risk is part of the thrill of successful living. No matter how successful you become, you will always long to fulfill your purpose. It's not the destination that brings you the satisfaction, it's the journey! Instinctively, you know this important truth, but the tricky part is living it out.

Reflective exercise

When have you achieved a major milestone in your life—a degree, a job, a promotion, a relational turning point—and felt disappointed that it didn't satisfy you the way you expected? How did you respond in that situation?

_____

_____

_____

Visualization

What's the biggest risk you would take in your life right now if you knew you couldn't fail? What's at stake if you take this leap and fail? What can you gain? Visualize yourself taking such an instinctive risk and achieving your goal successfully.

_____

_____

Practical exercise

Brainstorm and write a list of ten small risks you can take in the next week. These might include items like, "Ask Dr. Smith to lunch for advice about finishing my degree," or "Talk to my accountant about what's involved in launching my small business idea." Place a star next to five of these items and get started on at least one of them today.

_____

_____

"Your time is limited, so don't waste it living someone else's life. Don't be trapped by dogma—which is living with the results of other people's thinking. Don't let the noise of others' opinions drown out your own inner voice. And most important, have the courage to follow your heart and your intuition. They somehow already know what you truly want to become. Everything else is secondary."

—Steve Jobs (*Instinct*, p. 87)

CHAPTER 9

⬦

Your Instincts Under Pressure

You may feel tempted to lay low and hide in the back of the cage. When faced with the demands and pressures of life, you may not feel as if you have the energy and resources to take risks and start new ventures. With the stress of family responsibilities, work obligations, and financial burdens, you don't feel as if you have anything left over. Although your pace is different from mine and everyone else's, I challenge you to make risk taking a regular part of your instinctive lifestyle.

You will always face challenges in your life. There will always be family members who need your support, friends in crisis, deadlines at work, and financial obligations to be paid. You simply cannot allow yourself to ignore your risk-taking instincts while you wait for the right time. Life tends to spill over into all areas and require as much as you can give. But this doesn't mean that you don't step out in faith at crucial junctures by following your instincts.

The pressures and stressors you face each day may even indicate that you're overdue for a change! Sometimes it's more stressful staying in place and working to maintain status quo than facing your fears and embracing change. When you're guided by your instincts, you allow yourself more choices than if you just sit by and wait for life to happen to you. Being proactive, planning ahead, and anticipating opportunities are the results when you use life's pressures in productive ways.

Self-assessment exercise

What are the most stressful demands presently in your life? How do you usually handle stress? Where do you turn for relief, rest, and comfort?

_____

_____

Which relationships in your life currently require the most energy and attention? What dynamics would you change in these relationships if you could? What's preventing you from making these changes?

_____

_____

Self quiz

On the following scale, indicate how you usually respond to significant changes in your life:

1	2	3	4	5	6	7	8	9	10
	resistant			tolerant			eager		welcoming

What changes frighten or intimidate you the most? Changes in relationships at home? At work or in your career? In your finances? With your health? Others?

_____

_____

When have you unexpectedly benefited from a dramatic change in your life?
How did you discover the gift in the midst of your discomfort?

_____

_____

_____

Your Instincts Like a Challenge

Perhaps it's just your innate desire to survive or to make your own choices in life. Or maybe you simply feel as if you don't have a choice. When life crashes in on you, however, you do have choices—no matter what happens, you *always* have choices, even if they're very limited by circumstances. Maybe it's simply the fear of regret that motivates you to get back on your feet, take the next step, and resume your journey.

Regret can certainly be a powerful motivator, and your instincts know this. Most people, from research psychologists to ninety-year-old seniors, seem to agree that it's better to risk action and fail than to take no action and forever wonder "What if...?" When you choose not to risk, you must accept that you cannot know the results of what might have happened. So much of life is simply about showing up and engaging with the present moment and the opportunities that present themselves. If you don't take a leap of faith, then you must accept the unknown possibilities of what might have been.

Occasionally, you know that it's the right time to risk regardless of your circumstances. Changing careers, moving to a new location, or starting a relationship require enormous strength and courage. But if your instincts are guiding you, then you will eventually find yourself standing on the edge of a cliff with the notion to jump! Others may be there to support you, even to help catch you if you fall, but you alone are the only one who can step out of the cage and over the edge.

Pensive points

What important life decisions would you choose differently if you could make them over? Why would you change them? In other words, what do you regret about them?

_____

_____

Which do you usually regret more: what you do that fails or what you don't do that leaves you wondering what you missed? What do you regret most that you chose not to do in your life so far? What do you regret most that you've done?

_____

_____

What's the biggest leap of faith you've made toward improving your life? What consequences have emerged so far? What have you learned? What do your instincts tell you is the next step?

_____

_____

Your Instinct to Fly

While others cannot make your choices for you, sometimes they can give you a nudge! Like the mother bird that knows it's time for her babies to leave the nest and try out their wings, sometimes your loved ones must remind you that it's time to move on. Other times, your circumstances may necessitate a sink-or-swim, fly-or-die-trying response. When you lose your job and have no prospects on the horizon, it's time to fly. When your spouse divorces you and you have to provide for your children, it's time to fly. When you finally complete your degree, it's time to fly.

Although you have this instinct to soar, life often tries to beat it out of you. You become weary, scarred, wounded, and exhausted by all the demands and burdens placed upon you. You're tempted to stop risking, to stop caring, to stop trying, to stop hoping for anything more than what you've already experienced. You fear that the best has already been and all that remains is a downhill slide toward desperation. But this is simply not true!

If you follow your instinctive rhythm, then it's never too late to risk improving yourself. Oh, it may be tempting to believe that the beautiful, young, successful people are the only ones who fulfill their destiny, that your opportunities have already passed you by, but nothing could be further from the truth. Over time, your true character reveals itself and you're forced to strip away surface layers, or your ego-driven pretense, and follow your true instincts.

Maybe you already have regrets or wish you had made different choices. Fair enough, but what you've learned is priceless information about yourself, your desires, and your dreams. If you follow your instincts, it's never too late to succeed!

Research exercise

Surf on the web through travel sites and make a list of three places you've never been that you would love to visit someday. If you have the resources, choose one and begin planning a trip there later this year. If you currently don't have the means, then begin saving for such a trip, and in the meantime, download a free visitor's guide or purchase a travelogue about this place. Try to identify why it appeals to you.

_____

_____

Practical exercise

If you could change careers and do anything other than what you're presently doing, what field would you explore? What aspects of this career field appeal to you? Why? Do some sleuthing and try to find someone in your area who works in this other career area. Set up a time to interview them over coffee or at least have a phone conversation.

_____

_____

Self-acceptance exercise

If you could make one change to your body, what would it be? Why? Is this desired change due to what others think of you or something that comes from within? Or a combination of both? What do your instincts tell you about how to handle this aspect of yourself that you wish you could change? Accept it? Cover it up? Change what you can?

_____

_____

"There are times when we must disregard the data and distance our doubts if we are ever going to achieve greater velocity toward the goals that roar within us. We must follow our instinct to fly"

(*Instinct*, p. 101).

꘎

CHAPTER 10

Your Instincts Set the Pace

*Your instincts tell time better than
any clock or calendar.*

Sometimes your instincts compel you to run out of the cage, jump over the edge, and fly out of the nest. But as you've already realized, not all instinctive rhythms are the same. Often your gut instinct may be to wait until you have more capital to invest or until you have a partner in your entrepreneurial venture or until your health improves. Your instincts dispense wisdom about timing just as they inform you of what course of action to take. Your instincts know exactly the right time to wait and exactly the best time to act.

If you're attuned to them, often your instincts will help you make a transition in gradual stages. Instead of leaving your cage and slamming the door shut behind you, simply take a few steps beyond the threshold and look around before returning. The next time you can venture even farther until finally you are ready to remain free and can't imagine returning to the confinement of your former cage.

Whether you think of it as a safety net, a Plan B, or an escape hatch, it's instinctively wise to plan for contingencies. Sometimes these other options are where your instincts actually want to lead you. Other times, they're simply ways to safeguard your resources and provide peace of mind during a time of transition.

Reflective exercise

What's your natural instinctive pace when you take a risk? Do you tend to move quickly and sort through the consequences down the road? Or do you like to take your time and make slow, careful movements for each step along the way?

_____

_____

Introspective exercise

How do you interact with people whose instinctive rhythm is noticeably different from yours? Which type of person frustrates you more: The slowpoke who causes delays and bottlenecks? Or the speed freak who's always racing ahead and waiting on others to catch up?

_____

_____

Self-assessment exercise

How would you describe your current pace of life? Too fast? Too slow? Just right? What's required for you to attain more work-life balance right now?

_____

_____

_____

It's Your Move

During different seasons and circumstances of life, your instinctive rhythm changes. What might have started as a fast-paced, adrenaline-fueled leap of faith may settle into a slower, more even-keeled transition. You may make the decision to switch careers and accept a new job overnight, but then you must settle into handling the details of relocating, moving, and settling into your new position.

Some opportunities may carry an automatic deadline or be available only for a limited time. When forced to make a rather quick decision, you would do well to heed your instincts' call to wisdom as well as instructive pace. Perhaps you impose a sense of urgency where none exists. You might assume you must respond immediately, when you could receive more time if you simply asked for it. Knowing your own needs and keeping your true best interests front and center are instinctive priorities.

Most often the choices you make and the pace you set require a commitment. You can't undo them and go back to the way things used to be in your cage. This inability to retreat may even be a blessing in disguise at times. When confronted with initial resistance or early obstacles, you may tuck tail and run back to your doghouse instead of remaining on your own in the wild. While regrets may linger occasionally, your instincts have a keen sense of moving forward. You may try to replicate the past or repeat the same patterns of behavior, but your instincts naturally take you to new heights.

Assessment exercise

Have you ever experienced buyer's remorse about a decision and wish you could undo it? How did you handle the consequences? How has the decision impacted other choices you've made?

_____

_____

Reflective exercise

What patterns of behavior do you tend to repeat in life? Do you start getting restless and try to change jobs every five years? Do you find yourself returning to certain relationships, locations, or events on a regular basis?

_____

_____

Paired exercise

When have you had second thoughts about taking a certain action only to discover it was the right one over the long haul? Are you more inclined to base decisions on short-term consequences or long-term impact?

_____

_____

After considering your answers, talk with a trusted friend or family member about their observations of the way you usually make important decisions.

When You Stumble

Most expertise is earned the hard way—from trial and error. Through experimentation, midcourse corrections, the wise counsel of others with more experience, and perseverance, you gain a graduate degree in instinctive living. Sooner or later, you're bound to stumble; the trick is to make sure you fall forward!

Most instinctively successful people I know have attained their education through the school of hard knocks. Some have dropped out of college so they can travel and explore new options. Others have switched careers in midlife and failed dozens of times before cracking the code of their greatest success. Many have ended up in roles, careers, industries, and occupations that they never imagined a few years ago. But they've continued to stumble forward, taking advantage of each opportunity as it comes, opening each new door, getting up and going forward over and over again.

Yes, you will encounter the naysayers, critics, and pundits who would rather take shots at your attempts than risk anything themselves. And certainly not all criticism is harmful—much of it can help you improve areas of weakness and overcome liabilities that are dragging you down. But the attitude and intentionality of the person providing feedback reveals so much about their motives. If they truly want to encourage, support, and challenge you to fulfill your potential, then you will sense their constructive energy. However, if jealousy, envy, or competitive comparison fuels their motives, then you must steer clear of their intended destructive power.

Don't be afraid of the input others may offer you about your journey. Always listen when others offer you advice, feedback, or instruction. Thank them for their input and then consider it, assess it, and evaluate its worth. Ultimately, however, you can rely only on your own instincts and not anyone else's. You must move to the beat of your own drummer as you advance to the next stage of your instinctive success!

Review and reflect exercise

It's time for your midterm examination! Don't panic—if you've made it this far, you've already earned an A+ with a gold star! You simply need to review your answers, ideas, feelings, artistic expressions, and images in this practical application guide. Answer the following questions as quickly and honestly as you can. Remember, there's no way you can fail!

YOUR INSTINCT IN ACTION

How have your ideas about your personal instincts changed since you began reading *Instinct* and exploring this application guide?

_____

_____

_____

_____

What has surprised you most in what you discovered about yourself so far? What has confirmed what you already suspected?

_____

_____

_____

_____

Which of the previous ten chapters has spoken to you in the most powerful way? What ideas and feelings has it stirred inside you?

_____

_____

_____

_____

What big idea or radical change is brewing inside you right now? What are your instincts leading you to explore?

_____

_____

_____

Throughout the course of your day, how aware are you of your instincts operating now? How has this awareness improved your life?

_____

_____

_____

"It's not how many times you have failed; it's what you've learned each time you got back on your feet"

(*Instinct*, p. 110).

✣

CHAPTER 11

Your Instinctive Investments

When you're out of sync with your instincts, you may not realize that you've been pursuing the wrong goals for your fulfillment until you achieve them. The proverb about being careful what you wish for because you might get it often applies to your misguided efforts to find satisfaction in the souvenirs of success without having made the actual journey. Instinctive success savors the daily ups and downs, the failures and triumphs, the decisions and diversions, more than any corner office, trophy, or diploma on the wall.

If you've opened the channel to greater instinctive awareness, then you may be realizing that what you thought you wanted is only a mirage. However, the good news is that the true oasis you seek may be closer than you thought. You may be on an instinctive track toward what your heart truly desires, even as you experience a season of discontent chasing what others have placed before you. When you invest in your own unique instinctive success, you will find that you don't have to chase awards, affluence, or achievements. They will find you!

Self-assessment exercise

How do you presently measure and define your own personal success? What have you achieved or acquired in your life so far that's proof of your advancement? How does this evidence satisfy your instinct to increase? How does it inspire you to greater things?

_____

_____

Reflective exercise

What achievements or apparent successes have disappointed you or left you longing for more than what you attained? How have these disappointments influenced your definition of success?

_____

_____

Instinctive success exercise

What accomplishment, achievement, or work in progress has brought you the most personal satisfaction? What did you enjoy most about pursuing this goal? What did this pursuit bring out in you that other pursuits of success usually do not?

_____

_____

Your Instinct Multiplies Success

Jesus' parable of the talents remains one of the most relevant, insightful applications of instinctive success that I've ever encountered. While it's symbolically spiritual in its message, it's also highly practical and applicable to virtually all areas of our lives. In many ways, it's a variation of another biblical truth: "You reap what you sow" (see Galatians 6:7).

Scripture exercise

Read the parable of the talents in Matthew 25:14–30 in your favorite version of the Bible. As you read, consider which of the three servants' responses seems most like your own. How do you usually handle responsibility? How do you typically approach long-term plans that require significant investment? What truth from the parable applies most to your current situation?

_____

_____

_____

Jesus takes his cautionary tale about investments, consequences, and dividends beyond the "reap and sow" theme you might expect in the parable of the talents. In this story of a master going on a journey, you must choose your response to a universal and fundamental question of existence: what will you do with the treasure God has invested in you? And here in the parable, you really have only two responses. You either invest boldly and wisely and return more to the master than what he originally gave you; or you succumb to your fears and bury your treasure, returning no dividend on your master's investment, only the original capital.

The two servants who invested their master's money—or talents, as they're aptly called in Scripture—achieved an amazing promotion. "Well done, my good and faithful servant," the master says to them. "You're going to be placed in charge of more! Get your things, you're coming to stay with me." This notion was entirely radical for Jesus' audience! Slaves becoming masters? What in the world could God be trying to reveal about the nature of risking what we've been given?

On the other hand, the third servant failed in a way from which he could not recover. His plight reminds you of the ultimate regret, living a life in which you buried what you were entrusted to invest. Paralyzed by fearful, false perceptions of his master, this slave is called wicked and condemned for his tepid decision to play it safe. Yes, it seems clear that you have indeed been given an instinct to increase—it's only a matter of how you will use it.

Pensive points

What new theme or implication emerged from considering the parable of the talents within the context of an instinctive explication?

_____

_____

_____

What fears influence you to bury your talents rather than invest them? What are you afraid of happening if you risk fulfilling your own God-given potential? Are you more afraid of success or of failure?

_____

_____

_____

Practical exercise

In what area of your life do you presently need to dig up your buried treasure and invest it in something that can produce divine dividends? What have you been holding back that you instinctively need to release at this time in your life? What one change can you make today to help you risk more in the areas revealed by your instincts?

_____

_____

_____

Your Threshold of Success

Fear is a funny thing. It can paralyze you or it can motivate you. It can detach and derail you from your instinctive direction, or it can heighten the urgency and sensitivity of your instincts. Fear remains an inevitable part of life. Even the most courageous, brave, powerful, and valiant individuals get afraid at times. No, the fear experienced by the third slave in the parable is not the problem. It's his response to the fear that caused his failure.

Your fears will always attempt to infiltrate your insight and poison your potential. But you must acknowledge them without allowing them to determine your actions. I'm convinced the more you're in touch with your instinctive drive, the more powerfully you can overcome your fears. Your instincts know that if your fears are left unchecked they can destroy you, which goes against your strongest drive to survive.

You know in your heart of hearts that you were made for more than what you've achieved so far in life. Whether you're a beggar or a billionaire, you remain poised on the threshold of instinctive success. Don't bury the treasure you've been given because you're afraid of losing it. Ironically, the only way *not* to lose it is to invest it in something eternal—the fulfillment of your divine destiny.

Take the next risk that you must take to be a good steward of the treasure already inside you. The greatest satisfaction comes from the achievement of what God has created you and you alone to do on this earth. He's given you powerful instincts as your guide—it's time you unleashed them for the maximum return on his investment!

Memory challenge

When was the last time you felt the exhilaration of doing what you know you were uniquely created to do? What were the circumstances in this moment? What role did your instincts play in experiencing this kind of soul satisfaction?

_____

_____

_____

Talents inventory

Make a list of the talents, abilities, skills, and unique experiences you've discovered, developed, and accumulated in your life. Give each category a column and jot down as many in each category as you can.

_____

_____

_____

After you're satisfied with your lists for each—talents, abilities, skills, and unique experiences—evaluate how each category is currently being invested.

_____

_____

_____

Paired exercise

Choose someone you trust who knows you well, preferably for a long time. Schedule some time with this confidant and discuss your fears about the future with them. Let your friend know your thoughts and feelings in response to reading *Instinct* and discovering more about yourself through this practical application guide. Ask them to repeat back to you what they've heard you saying. Discuss with them anything that seems inaccurate or surprising.

> *"It's time for you to respond to the rapping fist of opportunity's*
> *fierce knock on the door of your life right now. If you will answer*
> *the knock and honor the chance with discipline, creativity,*
> *and urgency, you may find yourself—your true self—living*
> *a life that exceeds your wildest dreams!"*
>
> (*Instinct*, p. 131).

CHAPTER 12

Your Instincts Protect You from Predators

The same instincts that lead you to new levels of success will protect you from new threats.

Once you've taken a leap of faith and made a bold move, it's tempting to think that you've arrived at the next level. While your entrance into excellence should be celebrated, you must also be prepared to defend yourself and your core identity and beliefs as you encounter new people in your new environment.

Regardless of how kind, friendly, and helpful they may appear, others will accurately regard your arrival as a catalyst for change. At best, you will strike them as a curiosity that requires further scrutiny. At worst, your new community members will assess you as a threat to their own instinctive success.

Just as my Roman Cane Corsos, Bentley and Sable (mentioned on pages 133–135 of *Instinct*), learned the hard way that their new domain included prior inhabitants, you must engage with the new people around you without assuming the worst. You don't want to get off on the wrong foot because you're automatically projecting a defensive, accusatory attitude. But on the other hand, you don't want to let your guard down all at once. You want to lower the gate to your vulnerable self gradually and slowly, over time, as you get better acquainted with your new environment and its other inhabitants.

Self-assessment exercise

When you find yourself in new situations, how do you usually respond to new acquaintances? How would others describe their first impressions of you? Warm and friendly? Aloof and reserved? Direct and no-nonsense? Casual and collegial?

_____

_____

_____

Reflective exercise

Do you tend to err on the side of trusting people too much or not trusting them enough? How long does it typically take you to form an opinion or assessment of new people in your life?

_____

_____

_____

Instinctive awareness exercise

How accurate are your first impressions of other people? What role do your instincts play in forming these initial ideas of others' characters and personalities? Would you say that your instinctive assessment of others based on first impressions tends to be accurate most of the time, some of the time, or none of the time?

_____

_____

Prey for Your Predators

It's simply human nature to try to find your place when introduced into a new social system. When you arrive in a new environment, whether a new workplace, church committee, or community softball team, you enter into an atmosphere already infused with alliances and opinions, history and heresy, attitudes and outlooks.

Others may welcome you, enlist your support, or leave you cold, but everyone you encounter will definitely be analyzing and assessing you the same way you are sizing them up. Animals, of course, are the same way—sniffing each other, barking and biting, chasing and chewing—and sometimes much more!

The difference, however, is that animals typically do not pretend to regard each other one way and then act in the opposite manner. There's no pretense, deception, or subterfuge in the animal kingdom the way you sometimes encounter it in humanity! So you must hone your instincts in ways that help you discern others' motives, methods, and machinations the same way my dogs sniff the scent of a coyote on our property.

Obviously, the more time you spend together, the more data you have to assess these new members of your society. However, here more than anywhere, don't discount your instincts. If someone strikes you as untrustworthy, even though you have no basis for it, don't tell them anything you don't want repeated! Listen to your instinctive wisdom as it filters and familiarizes you with this new cast of characters in your life's latest chapter.

Memory challenge

When was the last time you were aware of being the newbie on the scene? What were the circumstances that led to your arrival? What were your first impressions of those around you?

_____

_____

_____

Self quiz

How would you describe your style of relating to other people? Look at the following pairs of words and choose the one in each pair that more accurately describes your relational style.

Introvert	Extrovert
Loud	Soft-spoken
Opinionated	Reserved
Analytic	Empathic
Gullible	Cynical
Conversational	Professional
Warm	Distant
Complicated	Transparent
Laid-back	Assertive
Black-and-white	Shades of gray

Self-awareness exercise

How do you usually respond when it's clear that others are evaluating you? Do you like to show off, or do you tend to retreat and surprise them later? Do you resist their attempts to interrogate you or sidetrack them with stories?

_____

_____

_____

Remember Your Instinctive Identity

When you're thrust into the dynamics of a new social environment, it's only natural to want to fit in and be accepted. However, you must be aware of the cost. Having lunch with one group may unknowingly alienate another. Assisting certain team members may unintentionally set a precedent for how you will relate to one another. Spend some time observing the lay of the land before you begin making alliances and creating patterns in your social structure.

You will also have to make sure you remain firmly aware of your true identity as you assimilate in new circles. If you're not in possession of your instinctive strengths, abilities, and limitations, then you will soon be following someone else's script. Without realizing it, you will discover yourself acting outside of character, saying what others want to hear or doing what they expect to be done.

While it's good to be accepted and respected, you want to make sure that it's for the right reasons. Doing whatever it takes just to fit in rarely earns anyone's respect in the long run. However, knowing your authentic self and asserting your instinctive identity in naturally confident ways will always command others' respect, if not their acceptance as well. Trusting your instincts remains one of the best ways to defend yourself against the pursuit of predators.

Instinctive awareness exercise

How would you describe your role or persona in each of the following social environments? Write down the first words that come to mind for all that apply.

Home:_____

Work:_____

Church:_____

School:_____

Community/Neighborhood:_____

Club or Team: _____

Other: _____

Application exercise

When have you felt attacked, betrayed, or preyed upon by others in a new environment? How did you handle such predatory behavior? How will you handle it the next time you experience a similar hostile environment?

_____

_____

_____

Reflective exercise

How has your identity been challenged in your present roles and responsibilities? Which arenas seem to be the most difficult in maintaining your authentic self?

_____

_____

_____

Practical exercise

Choose one or two quotations from your readings in *Instinct* or this application guide to copy onto index cards. Place them where you will see them every day as a reminder to be true to your core instinctive identity.

"If you lose your sense of who you are, you have nothing to which you can return. If you don't discover your passions, purpose, and power, then you will pursue the roles assigned by other people's scripts. You will lose the success afforded by new opportunities if you don't know your own priorities and preferences"

(*Instinct*, p. 142).

CHAPTER 13

꽁

Your Informed Instincts

*Your instincts operate most effectively
when fueled by information
related to the areas of your greatest
passion.*

Your instincts operate most accurately and effectively when they combine your external data with your internal filters of emotion, experience, and expectation. When you rely on either sector exclusively—facts without feelings, or instincts without info—you severely limit your instinctive ability to succeed. Life constantly provides you with information, and at times you may feel overwhelmed by all the options, opinions, and operations competing for your attention. Simply put, you can't take it all in, but the good news is that you don't have to.

One of the great advantages of living instinctively is allowing your internal wisdom to filter and sort information for you. Many neurologists and psychologists have observed the way your brain's reticular activating system, a collection of nuclei performing many complex transitions, becomes stimulated when you encounter something that interests you. It's that experience you've probably had where you're trying to decide which car to buy, and suddenly all you notice on the highway is the model you want to purchase. It's why some articles in a magazine catch your attention and engage your thoughts while you skip over others altogether.

It's fascinating to consider the way your mind and body work harmoniously with your instincts. Part of what makes your instincts so powerful is their ability to synthesize a variety of source information, including ones that you may not consciously recognize as sharing common elements or relationships.

When you inform your instincts, you provide fuel for the passions, desires, and dreams burning within you. Make sure you don't neglect the significance of what you can learn from the facts—not just the information they impart but also how they relate to all the other areas of your instinctive knowledge.

Research assessment exercises

When you want to research a topic, where do you begin? What sources usually provide you with the most factual information? Which digital sources— websites, blogs, news sites, and forums—do you frequent most often? How reliable or trustworthy are these sources? What's the basis for their authority and credibility?

_____

_____

Why do these particular sources that you listed above appeal to you more than other similar sources that basically provide the same information? Are there certain styles, techniques, graphics, or audio effects that engage you more than others?

_____

_____

What other sources of information, news, and interviews do you usually read? Which magazines, periodicals, and journals? Which TV news programs, talk shows, and inspirational series?

_____

_____

Get Your Bearings

In order to inform your instincts, you must determine what you need to know. You must be able to examine your areas of knowledge and identify ones that require more information. Or, it might be updating education or expertise that you already possess. Most professions require you to stay up-to-date with the latest developments, products, trends, and methods in your field. In order to function effectively, your instincts need the same kind of ongoing informational input.

Also, as you get your bearings by recognizing your limitations and boundaries, keep in mind that your instinctive education is dynamic and ever evolving. You never arrive and stop learning. There's never going to be a point where you have mastered any subject so perfectly that there's nothing left to discover. The areas of interest that truly attract and engage you will only continue to deepen your passion. Which explains why the best experts are often those people who realize that the more they learn, the more there is to learn!

Affirmation

What educational experiences have had the greatest impact on your instincts? What training has proven to be the most valuable on a daily basis? Write an affirmation focused on what you've learned in life (or some part of your life's education) that continues to shape your instincts. For example, you might write, "Going back to school while working full-time showed me that I instinctively know how to per-severe. I am someone who never quits!"

_____

_____

_____

Visualization

Imagine that an intern or apprentice is shadowing you throughout your day. What would this student learn about what you do that cannot be taught in the classroom? What wisdom or advice would you pass along to this person about how to be successful?

_____

_____

_____

Research exercise

In what areas do you want to learn more? What educational areas, job training, and professional development skills in your repertoire need updating? Make a short list of these areas and opportunities, and choose one to research and pursue at this time in your life.

_____

_____

_____

Study Your Own Habits

Everyone has his or her own ways of learning, and becoming aware of how you assimilate information most effectively is crucial to your instinctive education. If you know you don't have the patience to scrutinize financial data, then you need to extract that information in other ways. If you know that reading reports makes you fall asleep, then you need another method of grasping the facts and findings. If you know you need graphics, graphs, charts, and other visuals, then let those around you know your preference. If hearing reports explained in a conversation helps you comprehend more efficiently, then find someone who can converse.

When you know your own instinctive habits, you liberate yourself to work more effectively. Are you a night owl and get energized after dinner? Do you work best as the sun comes up and find yourself drained by midafternoon?

Knowing the environmental factors that affect your educational success is also crucial. You want to maximize your opportunities to learn by controlling the variables within your reach. Don't underestimate the power of your learning environment. Colors, sounds, lights, movement, and texture all have an impact on how you engage and process information. Discover what works best for you and use it to your advantage.

Self-awareness exercise

How would you describe your learning style? Visual? Audial? Hands-on? A combination? When have you enjoyed learning the most? What factors contributed to your positive learning experience?

_____

_____

_____

Visualization

Imagine that you have a huge report to write and present to a room full of prospective clients. Assuming you had all the informational resources you needed, what would your ideal learning environment look like?

Be as specific as possible:

☐ What color are the walls?

☐ What kind of music is playing?

☐ Or is it a silent environment?

☐ Are you alone?

☐ Or are other people nearby?

☐ Are you sitting?

☐ Standing?

☐ Laying down?

☐ Outside?

☐ In a cozy corner?

☐ Or an expansive area?

☐ What other details do you see?

_____

_____

_____

Focusing on such minute details may seem silly or irrelevant, but if you pay attention to what works best for you, it's surprising how easily you can often control and manipulate these variables and improve your retention, comprehension, and performance.

Research exercise

Make a list of topics, ideas, people, places, and events that you would like to know more about for no reason other than your own curiosity. Choose one, either the most useful or the most intriguing, to begin researching right away. Do more than an online search. Visit a library, bookstore, classroom, or museum. Find an expert, if possible, and ask them to explain their passion for what you're researching.

_____

_____

_____

_____

_____

Graphic visualization exercise

Using images you find online, as well as in magazines, greeting cards, art prints, and other creative sources, look for elements of your ideal learning environment, a special room that's yours alone. Whether you call it a study, an office, a lounge, or a library, choose colors, designs, and details that would facilitate your greatest instinctive education. Now paste, sketch, draw, and paint these different elements into a scene you can keep in front of you during the day. Bonus points if you can put all the details together so that they actually look like your dream room!

Self-assessment exercise

What course do you need to take, which test do you need to pass, how much training do you need to sharpen your instincts in the area of your greatest passion? Take one action toward acquiring this instinctively essential information.

_____

_____

"If you don't find a way to enhance your instinct through research, you forfeit the opportunity to belong"

(*Instinct*, p. 150).

CHAPTER 14

⬦

Your Instinctive Leadership

When you live instinctively, the opportunity
for leadership will naturally present itself.

In moving closer to your dreams and instinctive success, you will take on more responsibilities as your endeavors expand and reach fruition. Sooner or later, you will need to enlist others in the process of fulfilling your instinctive desires, and that requires leading them forward as only you can. Eventually, you will look up and realize that everyone else is looking to you for direction!

You may be intimidated by the notion of considering yourself a leader, or it may come naturally to you. When you live instinctively, leadership may not resemble what corporate manuals and business textbooks describe, but it will come naturally nonetheless. You may be surprised to learn that what you fear is based on misperceptions and even more surprised to discover that what you're already doing demonstrates leadership.

You might assume leaders must have all the answers, be comfortable speaking before large groups, and know how to dress like an executive out of *Vogue* or *GQ*. These stereotypical qualities are rarely what determine an effective, instinctively successful leader, however. Instinctive leaders know that ultimately it's not how they look, sound, or even what they may say. Instinctive leadership is about taking responsibility for the fulfillment of your goals.

This instinctive achievement may require collaboration, synchronization, and delegation with three people or three thousand—in fact, the more successfully you progress, the more these relational components may multiply. But regardless of how big or how successful you become in pursuit of your dreams, as an instinctive leader you will know how to remain focused.

Sure, you may stray and explore new areas that lead nowhere from time to time—after all, instinctive leaders take risks—but most of the time you'll be keenly focused on what you do best. Why? Because your instincts are guiding you in how you guide others!

Reflective exercise

Do you usually think of yourself as a leader? In all arenas or just certain ones? In which areas do you feel most comfortable leading others? How much experience have you had leading in these areas?

_____

_____

_____

What intimidates or frightens you most about leading other people? What do you enjoy most about it? Why?

_____

_____

_____

Role model exercise

Name the leaders you've served who have had the greatest impact on you and your leadership style. What did you learn from them? How has it influenced the way you lead others?

_____

_____

Your Style of Leadership

One of the fundamental tensions you will inevitably face as a leader, both within yourself and your organization, emerges from the clash of tradition and innovation. As an instinctive leader, you must learn quickly how to walk the tightrope between these two foundational pillars of sustained success.

On one end of the spectrum, you must acknowledge and respect what has occurred prior to your arrival in a new arena. And on the other end, you must be willing to risk doing things very differently in order for advancement and healthy growth to take place. This tension applies to virtually every area, from the people you lead (and let go) to the clients you serve and the methods you utilize.

If you want to make sure that you never achieve more than what you've accomplished presently, then keep doing things the exact same way. And if you want to make sure there's a legacy remaining beyond your leadership, then don't take any risk that jeopardizes the foundational focus of your enterprise. Instinctive leaders know that you can't ignore either of these parallel pillars supporting the underpinnings of your organization in order to succeed.

Therefore, these inherent tensions require you to discover an instinctive rhythm that accommodates both ingredients. Understanding tradition is often vital to identity, purpose, and continuity. If you don't grasp the essence of your brand, then you can't expand it and move it forward. Yet pursuing innovation is just as vital in the areas of relevance, progress, and growth. If you remain where you are, you soon grow stagnant and decay, going backward instead of forward. Your instincts can help you negotiate with both tradition and innovation, remaining aware of the changing needs and adapting at the right time.

Self-awareness exercise

As a leader, are you pulled more toward maintaining tradition or pursuing innovation? Does your default setting tend to leave something alone as long as it's working? Or do you like to explore change just to see if you can make things even better?

_____

_____

_____

Memory challenge

When have you felt squeezed between tradition and innovation? How did you handle the pressure? How did this experience influence your leadership instincts?

_____

_____

_____

Goal setting exercise

What's one thing you'd like to change in the current domain of your leadership? What has prevented you from changing it already? What's one thing you would like to ensure remains the same in the present arena where you lead? How can you protect it moving forward?

_____

_____

_____

Let Your Instincts Lead

In order to lead instinctively, you must be aware of your natural default tendencies and preferences in how you make decisions and communicate them, and in how you work with team members for their implementation and execution. When harnessed to the engine of your instincts, no one leadership style is necessarily better than another. My own style of leadership is what I call consultative. I like consulting as many stakeholders as possible as well as informing my decisions with as much factual data as possible. I have no problem being decisive, but I tend to move at my own instinctive pace rather than be pressured to draw premature conclusions.

Each and every unique style works well when aligned with a talented, hardworking individual's instincts. All styles include certain strengths and advantages as well as weaknesses and blind spots.

Leadership style self-assessment

Circle the words below that you feel are traits of your leadership.

☐ controlling
☐ accessible
☐ captivating

- ☐ charismatic
- ☐ charming
- ☐ communicative
- ☐ confident
- ☐ conversational
- ☐ decisive
- ☐ detached
- ☐ empowering
- ☐ equitable
- ☐ forceful
- ☐ independent
- ☐ invested
- ☐ motivating
- ☐ personal
- ☐ preoccupied
- ☐ proactive
- ☐ progressive
- ☐ respectful
- ☐ responsible
- ☐ team-oriented
- ☐ unifying
- ☐ unpredictable
- ☐ visionary

Based on the traits you circled, you may be able to identify yourself in the types below, or you may see yourself as a kind of unique hybrid of several styles.

Autocratic Style: controlling, independent, decisive, forceful, confident, responsible

Chaotic Style: empowering, accessible, team-oriented, conversational, unpredictable

Democratic Style: unifying, invested, equitable, proactive, respectful

Laissez-faire Style: motivating, visionary, progressive, preoccupied, detached

Persuasive Style: captivating, charming, charismatic, personal, communicative

Each leadership style incudes numerous strengths as well as an area of struggle. What do you see as your greatest leadership attributes? In other words, what do you do best, based on the way you lead others?

What areas need improvement? Where do you struggle the most in the way you lead others? For example, you may be a great communicator but have trouble dealing with personal conflicts.

Strong instinctive leaders often possess many of these characteristics in some form of hybrid style. They use their instinctive sensibilities to know which qualities are needed to produce the desired results at the proper time. These leaders know that you must adapt and step outside your natural tendencies in order for others to invest in your mission and follow you.

When you lead instinctively, you also know that you will have to become adept at reading between the lines. From résumés to quarterly reports, often the most important messages emerge from what is not on the page. Many social skills and personality strengths will not be reflected on an applicant's résumé. Budget reports and marketing updates need to be translated into more accessible language for various stakeholders.

You simply can't reduce instinctive leadership to a standard formula or a series of steps. Leading successfully requires a keen awareness of your instincts, a willingness to trust in your own inner wisdom, and the courage to take full responsibility. As you develop into a more instinctive leader, look for opportunities to stretch your abilities and follow where your instincts lead. You may be surprised how many others will follow!

Role model exercise

Make a list of the leaders you admire and respect the most. Consider various areas of your life and community, not just your workplace. Include government leaders, church leaders, historical leaders, military leaders, industry leaders, leaders of social change, and personal mentors. Make note of any common denominators that they all share in their leadership styles.

_____

_____

_____

Practical exercise

Choose someone from your list of admired leaders, probably someone local whom you know, and make an appointment with them. Let them know that you admire the way they lead and want to learn from them. Think through at least three questions you want to ask them during your meeting.

_____

_____

_____

Research exercise

Choose a famous, well-known, or historical leader from your admired-leaders list and read a biography of this person. Make notes about this person and what surprises you about their life. In what ways are you already like this instinctive leader?

_____

_____

_____

"Inspirational leaders ignite a spark within us that compels us to be part of the blaze they are lighting. When you inspire people to come on board with you, you are evolving into an instinctive leader"

(*Instinct*, p. 170).

CHAPTER 15

Your Instincts Don't Stink!

*Your mistakes provide opportunities
to sharpen your instincts.*

Maybe you've heard the saying, "Your best decisions have gotten you to where you are right now." It's one I've heard said when someone expresses their dissatisfaction with their current status, meaning that they have played a part—a large part—in arriving at their present destination. Many life circumstances are certainly beyond your control, but how you respond to them is well within your instinctive grasp. Your past mistakes and present flaws may reveal more about your instincts than your achievements and talents.

While your instincts aren't always accurate, rarely do they lead you totally astray. They turn the decisions, failures, and disappointments of your life into opportunities. And if you're willing to sift through the painful areas of your life, the tender areas where you continue to feel vulnerable, then your instincts can help you heal and move forward much more quickly and effectively.

Reflective exercise

What personal mistake or bad decision has provided you with the most insight into your weaknesses? What prompted you to make this misstep at the time? Whether it was last week or years ago, as you look back now, what have you learned about yourself from this messy experience?

_____

_____

Self-assessment exercise

How much responsibility do you take for your choices and actions in life? When you're honest with yourself, do you allow yourself to play the victim? Or do you embrace the options you do have, regardless of how limited they may be, and make the most of moving forward?

_____

_____

Memory challenge

What's one mistake you've made that's turned out to have a silver lining? How has it influenced your instinctive choices since?

_____

_____

Make Your Mistakes Your Motivations

The wounds of your past failures often motivate you more than you realize. When you become fixated only on what you did wrong, blaming yourself and others, you end up bitter instead of better. Instead of learning as much as you can from life's discouraging incidents, you end up getting trapped in them. You may wonder why you cannot seem to move forward and yet continue to cling to something that happened a long time ago.

As a result of your bitterness, regret, and disappointment over what you've lost, you run away from present opportunities rather than risk experiencing the same outcomes. Or, you refuse to look at your motives, emotional baggage, and needs, and you find yourself repeating patterns that only leave you stuck, basically repeating past mistakes. You may instinctively know that in order to truly heal and move forward you must take responsibility for what you can and release what's beyond your control.

Many people ask me why they seem to be attracted to the same kind of person over and over again, always with the same painful results. Investors and entrepreneurs will sometimes inquire why I think they continue to struggle, fail, and have to start again. Individuals battling addictions also know this feeling, a sense of being caught in a cycle of futility, frustration, failure, from which they cannot find a way to escape.

It's never easy, but your instinctive desire to survive and to thrive can help you break these patterns if you let them. But you must be willing to step back and look at those messes and mistakes with a more objective, critical perspective. You must be willing to look within and assess what needs are going unmet—as well as what payoff you're getting for remaining trapped in this cycle.

God has gifted his human creations with intellect, insight, and instinct so that we can be higher than the animals. He has instilled a spiritual dimension, often called the soul, as an integral part of your being. You are an amazing, unique, and eternal creature.

Scripture search

Using your favorite concordance or online search tool, find three Bible verses that indicate how "wonderfully and fearfully" you've been made.

_____

_____

_____

_____

You don't have to keep repeating the mistakes of the past, running from your painful mistakes, or spinning your wheels in frustration. If you use your instincts as a tool, much as a scientist uses a microscope, you can see beyond the surface and make lasting changes in the right direction. You can instinctively grow into the mature, successful individual God created you to be.

Forgiveness exercise

Identify the major wounds that have been inflicted on you by others—your parents, family of origin, spouse, children, teachers and coaches, close friends, and business associates. How have you pursued forgiveness and healing from these setbacks? What have you learned about yourself from these injuries to your soul?

_____

_____

_____

_____

Self-assessment exercise

Identify the major wounds that you have inflicted on others—perhaps some of the same people who have hurt you deeply, as well. Who do you still need to ask for forgiveness? What other lingering effects and consequences must be addressed before you are free to move forward?

_____

_____

_____

Memory challenge

What incidents, accidents, and events in your life embarrass you or cause you the most shame? What secret are you holding that continues to short-circuit your instinctive drive for success? What needs to happen to break free of the hold these areas have on your life?

_____

_____

_____

Making Room for Your Instincts to Operate

If you truly want to change your life and to experience the abundant satisfaction that comes from living instinctively, then you must be willing to examine the wreckage of past mistakes and clear the scene of the accident. Just as a car crash can block the highway for hours, your collisions often impede your ability to move forward into your destiny. Instead of doing the hard work that has to be done to clear the wreckage and begin again, you remain burdened by a past you can never change.

However, you can change the future by taking responsibility and making steps toward instinctive advancement in your present. Often this process requires that you let go of old baggage, heal from past injuries, and make room for the new growth awaiting your arrival. As long as you're clinging to the old mistakes and past disappointments, you likely don't have room to welcome the new changes your instincts want to bring into your life.

Sometimes you literally have to clear the clutter of the past from your life, getting rid of items that may have once served a purpose but now only get in your way. Often there's emotional baggage that must be unpacked and released. Almost always, there are changes to be made in how you spend your time each day. You must make room for your instincts to operate if you want to heed their wisdom and break free from the prison of the past.

Paired exercise

Have at least one conversation that you need to have in order to release yourself from past pain. It may mean asking someone you've hurt for forgiveness or granting forgiveness to someone who has hurt you. It may mean discussing an incident or event with another person who can provide you with some clues about your own behavior at the time. You may need to share a secret struggle with someone and begin the process of seeking the help you need.

Make a list of what you consider your worst moments or greatest mistakes. After you've spent a few minutes compiling your list, go back through it and indicate any positive consequences that have emerged from these painful moments. Place a star next to the items on your list for which you cannot see any positives. These areas still need to be examined, addressed, and healed before you can benefit from your instinctive power to succeed.

Worst Moments/Greatest Mistakes	Positive Consequences
_____	_____
_____	_____
_____	_____

Areas Identified That Still Need Healing:

_____

_____

_____

Paired exercise

Have lunch or dinner with a close friend whom you trust. Ask them to share one of their life's mistakes and how they've processed it in exchange for your own confession. Help your friend see the way that this mistake has benefited them in at least one way; ask them to do the same with yours.

"When you burn off the clutter of busyness and leave yourself time to think and study, you may get less done, but the things you do will be far more productive and ultimately more organic to what you are passionate about accomplishing"

(*Instinct*, p. 190).

CHAPTER 16

✠

Balancing Your Intellect and Your Instinct

Your head and your heart produce amazing offspring—your instincts.

Your mind craves knowledge and often prefers facts that can be attained and verified from reliable sources. Your heart seeks emotional connections and experiential wisdom that may not be quantifiable but is nonetheless as truthful as any verifiable fact. When your head and your heart compare notes, the results often emerge in your instincts. Therefore, in order for your instincts to be as well informed and sharply focused as possible, you need to make sure you are actively including both the mental and emotional dimensions of your being. You cannot neglect either area and expect your instincts to operate at full capacity.

You must perform the due diligence and research necessary to inform your decisions and actions. You must search inside yourself for the passions, desires, and attractions that fulfill your divinely appointed potential. Together, your intellect and instincts join hands and work harmoniously to carry you toward the success and satisfaction that neither could approach alone. Keeping the necessity of this balancing act as a priority, you empower your instincts to be twice as strong.

Memory challenge

Are you usually led more by your head or your heart? Think of a significant recent decision that illustrates your choice.

_____

_____

_____

How do you usually use your intellect to provide "checks and balances" on your instincts? How do you typically filter your intellectual assessments through your instincts?

_____

_____

_____

Self-awareness exercise

What's the most challenging aspect of balancing your intellect and your instincts? How often does one tend to run ahead of the other in your experience?

_____

_____

_____

Your Balancing Acts

Finding balance between your intellect and your instincts often requires you to rely on your relationships. When you include people with different points of view, different biases and preferences, and different informational angles in your conversations, you're instinctively seeking balance. If you surround yourself only with people who reinforce what you already believe, then you're not going to strike the balance you need in order to see clearly.

Similarly, you must be keenly aware of your own blind spots. Everyone has weaknesses, and these must be taken into account as you find the right tempo for the dance between your intellect and instincts. You cannot ignore what you don't know, and you can't assume that it won't bite you—eventually it will! So you must bring in people, perspectives, and points of view that help you see what you cannot see on your own.

In football, quarterbacks know that when they turn to throw a pass, they always have a blind side. If their offensive line cannot cover this blind side by holding off defenders, then the quarterback will find himself lying on his back looking up! Without someone protecting you from what you can't see, the door is open to predators and manipulators. Finding your balance requires coverage in a 360-degree rotation.

Role model exercise

Think about the three individuals you would go to right now if you had a major decision to think through. Are these three people more similar to one another or more different from one another? What can each one uniquely contribute to your attempt to find a balance between intellect and instinct?

_____

_____

Reflective exercise

What are your blind spots? In which areas do you tend to overlook, ignore, or underestimate important perspectives? Do your emotions sometimes blind you to the facts? Does your fear of risk cause you to take too long in making crucial decisions? What areas require additional attention as you make decisions and take actions to move forward?

_____

_____

_____

Practical exercise

Who's got your back? Literally, who are the people in your life who help you see things from every angle? Are there people you need to bring in so that you have full coverage for your vulnerabilities and blind spots? Who? Make plans to have conversations with at least two people who can help you be more aware of your blind spots.

_____

_____

_____

Your Instinctive Flexibility

Like a tightrope walker, a trapeze artist, or an experienced gymnast, you must remain agile if you are to maintain an ongoing balance between intellect and instinct. Such flexibility requires you to monitor all variables of your environment as closely as possible and to adapt accordingly. If the wind's blowing too much, don't get on the high wire!

Sometimes you have to wait until the various pieces align before moving forward with an opportunity. Sometimes you have to act immediately without hesitating to seize an opportunity before it disappears. Balancing your intellect with your instincts can help you know the difference.

Preparations and projections also provide the ballast you need to maintain your agility, flexibility, and adaptability. Just as new parents wouldn't bring a baby home without making preparations ahead of time, you must ensure you have what you need in advance whenever possible. When you've done your homework and prepared for as many contingencies as possible, then you have the freedom to improvise. To be more accurate, you will have more resources, information, and data with which you can improvise.

Finding balance between your ideas and inclinations, your plans and possibilities, requires a conscious awareness and respect for both your head and your heart. Factual information will always remain a valuable commodity as you seek to make decisions and execute your plans. But they tell only half the story. You must also exercise your instincts in order to know how to interpret the facts, how they compare to other pieces of information, including others' perspective on them.

Facts alone will never provide you with what you need to succeed. Nor will your instincts. Allow the two—your intellect and our instincts—to converse together frequently, regularly, and openly. They won't always align, nor should they. The points of friction, conflict, or concern between them often become your most revealing insight.

Interactive exercise

In *Instinct*, I describe two women who are both valued friends of mine, even though they have opposing opinions on most topics. Their value in helping me find balance between intellect and instincts remains invaluable. Identify two friends, acquaintances, or associates from your circle who probably come at life from very different perspectives. Invite them both to join you for a meeting to discuss an idea you would like to develop more fully. Listen carefully to what each one has to say.

_____

_____

Pensive points

When have you experienced a conflict between your intellect and your instincts? How did you respond to this apparent impasse? How did you find balance between them for moving forward?

_____

_____

Application exercise

Choose an area of your life where you're currently contemplating your next move. Instead of a "pros and cons" list, make an "intellect and instincts" list for your possible directions going forward. Which side has more points listed, "intellect" or "instincts"? What steps do you need to take to find balance between them before taking action?

_____

_____

"As essential as instincts are to exploring the design of your destiny, you must not ignore the facts for the feelings!"

(*Instinct*, p. 193).

❈

CHAPTER 17

Your Instinctive Relationships

Your instincts will often lead you to unexpected, worthwhile relationships.

You have likely become aware of noticing other people who move to an instinctive rhythm similar to your own. Your shared values, goals, and instinctive methods of solving problems often draw you to these individuals. They are often the ones you need in order to build a supportive and effective team.

However, you must also recognize that your instincts will often lead you to relationships outside your natural networks. The more you experience instinctive successes in new territories, the more you will encounter animals you may not have met before! After a new promotion, you may find yourself faced with colleagues from a whole new department of your company. When starting a small business, you will be forced to interact with local leaders in this industry within your community. When you volunteer to serve on the committee at church, you may not have realized how many new faces would be serving alongside you.

Sometimes these intersections can be intimidating or even frightening. But if your instincts are guiding you, these new interactions will usually be fruitful as well. Stop to consider this thought for a moment: if you only remain among a homogenous group of similarly minded individuals, then you can advance only as far as your shared overlapping abilities can take you. However, exposure and encounters with wildly diverse people can stimulate, inspire, and ignite new ideas, fresh perspectives, and additional resources. You need new relationships and exposure to diverse groups of people in order to sharpen your instincts and to further your abilities.

Rather than trying to insulate yourself or expanding your network with others similar to yourself, you should instinctively seek out those people who are different—sometimes radically different—from you. This may include people from different sectors of life, other professions, unique backgrounds, and diverse cultures. These people might come from different ethnic, socioeconomic, or educational backgrounds than your own. They bring a fresh and different perspective to the way you see life.

Consider this analogy: when you consistently remain in the same geographic area, you soon find it so familiar that you stop paying attention. You've established its parameters and know what you're going to find around most corners. However, when you go to a place or city that you've never visited before, your senses are heightened and you notice everything! The more different this locale is from home, the more likely you are to note and appreciate the differences! Meeting new people and stretching beyond your familiar comfort zone of relationships can stimulate your instincts with the same creative and dynamic impact.

Evaluation exercise

Think about the people with whom you'll be interacting today. Are the majority of these individuals more similar to you or more different? What do you have in common with each one? What's the most striking difference you have with each one?

_____

_____

Memory challenge

How do you usually respond to others who are vastly different from you? Recall the last time you met someone with striking differences. Were they naturally curious? Intimidated? Afraid? Uncertain? Annoyed? Something else?

_____

_____

Self-awareness exercise

What biases and prejudices are you aware of holding against others who may be different from you? How did these attitudes develop in you? What steps do you need to take in order to release them so that you become more accepting of others' differences?

_____

_____

Scripture exercise

Find at least two Bible verses or passages that demonstrate how God wants you to respond to others who may be different from yourself. You may begin by considering the inclusive nature of the Gospel. Jesus made it clear that the Good News is for male and female, rich and poor, young and old.

_____

_____

Cast Your Net

While you may sometimes feel intimidated or self-conscious when interacting with people who are different from those you're used to encountering, it's also very stimulating. Your instincts often borrow transferable ideas and associations from other fields in order to reach innovative discoveries and inventions. Without exposure to diverse interests and varied abilities, you're limiting your instincts' ability to do what they do best. Since you can never predict where your instincts might find inspiration, you must allow yourself to stretch beyond your relational comfort zone. In fact, I recommend that you actively seek out diverse individuals with whom you can exchange ideas, explore options, and exploit mutually beneficial opportunities.

When you cast a wide net to build your network, you're opening channels that may otherwise go ignored or be dismissed. Once you begin to experience the benefits of this expansive and instinctive way to build your relationships, you'll understand why they are so vitally important to fulfilling your potential for success. Whether you realize it or not, you're limited by your background, education, culture, and social climate. In order to see beyond them, you must allow yourself to engage with others who don't do things the same way you do.

Reflective exercise

Who is the most diverse, unique individual in your current network, someone who's very different from you in a number of ways? How did you meet this person? How would you describe your relationship with them? When was the last time you experienced a conversation with them?

_____

_____

Self-assessment exercise

When have you benefited from the input of someone very different from yourself? What were the circumstances that led to this encounter? What did you learn about yourself? About the other person?

_____

_____

_____

Memory challenge

When was the last time you traveled outside your usual territories and visited a new place? Whether it was a different neighborhood in your city or the country-side of a foreign country, what struck you about this different place? How did it influence your instincts upon returning home?

_____

_____

_____

Your Instincts Beyond Borders

In order for your instincts to carry you beyond the borders of your own self-imposed barriers, you must consider the different aspects of instinctive relationships. Four important principles can help you expand your abilities to interact with others. Let's quickly review them.

Inspiration: The differences and dissonance between what you know and what you encounter in other distinct individuals often stirs your imaginations into action. The greater the differences, the better you can see beyond your own limitations.

Intersections: You frequently cross paths with individuals who are vastly different from yourself. Each intersection is an opportunity for you to expand your instinctive vision and sharpen your instinctive abilities.

Integration: Once you encounter the differences of others, how do you then put what you've observed into practice? When you recognize and identify the mutual benefits, then you can pursue shared goals of instinctive action.

Execution: Regardless of whom you meet or what you learn from their differences, your instinctive drive will not improve or accelerate without your taking action. You must transform your inspiration, intersection, and integration into action if you want to succeed.

As you become more comfortable allowing your instincts to guide you, they will inevitably lead you beyond the familiar into new opportunities. The participants will be different, which in itself provides you with new possibilities and fresh perspectives. Don't allow fear, prejudice, or discomfort with the unfamiliar to rob you of the precious gift of instinctive relationships. Cast your nets wide and enjoy the new fish in your network!

Interactive exercise

Seek out an opportunity to encounter other people with interests, backgrounds, and priorities vastly different from your own. It may mean attending a group meeting, an ethnic cultural center, a university classroom, a barbershop or beauty parlor, or a church Bible study. Meet and mingle with as many people as possible, and choose at least one with whom you exchange contact information for a follow-up meeting.

YOUR INSTINCT IN ACTION

Research exercise

Explore a culture from a country other than the one in which you were born, ideally one that intrigues you and that you've always wanted to learn more about. After researching it online, describe what interests you about this culture and its people and customs. Illustrate your description with at least one image, photo, or sketch of something unique and iconic from this culture.

_____

_____

_____

Exploration exercise

Plan a trip within your budget that will take you to a place you've never visited. It could be a suburb in the area where you live, or it could be an exotic locale that you've dreamed of exploring. Set a date and begin preparing for this instinctive excursion.

> *"An instinct without execution is only a regret....We need other people—more than just the usual suspects. Extend your net and make it work in new and instinctive ways—you might be surprised what you can catch!"*
>
> (*Instinct*, p. 218).

✦

CHAPTER 18

Juggling with Your Instincts

*Success requires juggling, and juggling
successfully relies on instincts.*

Your to-do lists never seem to get any shorter. With seemingly more and more to be accomplished each day, you are constantly encouraged to multitask, multitrack, and multiply your efforts. However, as you become instinctively led, you will soon discover that not all juggling is created equal! Sometimes you're juggling the wrong balls in the air. You're taking on projects, tasks, and obligations that you instinctively know are not in your sweet spot. As uncomfortable as it may feel to disappoint others, your instincts can help you form important boundaries if you follow them.

Self-awareness exercise

What are the areas that you're currently juggling? Which ones should you allow to drop so that you can make room for new instinctive additions?

_____

_____

On the other hand, your instincts will also cause you to pick up new items to juggle along the journey of pursuing your best life. With each new opportunity and instinctive achievement, you may have more to know, see, touch, do, research, find, and execute on a daily basis. While it's certainly challenging, if it's truly instinctively directed, then your passion for fulfilling your life's purpose will satisfy, energize, and sustain you. When you're doing a lot of things all at once for the right reasons, juggling can be enjoyable.

Prioritization exercise

Prioritize the things you're currently juggling in your life. What responsibility is most important to you? And what's next after it? And then? Does the way you spend each day juggling reflect these priorities?

_____

_____

_____

Reflective exercise

What do you enjoy most about the things you're presently juggling? How are you benefiting from each one? Once again, are there some that you need to remove from your juggling routine?

_____

_____

_____

Juggling Is Timing

Jugglers know that they must remain focused, engaged, and active in order to keep all the chainsaws in the air. Once you begin living more instinctively, you will become more adept at taking risks as well as knowing which ones to take at which times. This sense of discernment is crucial to your instinctive advancement. Again, notice how important timing, pacing, and rhythm are to following your instincts successfully.

This innate sense of timing will also guide you progressively as you navigate toward your goals. Think about the old Tarzan movies and cartoons, and how he would swing from vine to vine in order to traverse the jungle. Like an experienced trapeze artist, you must also keep your hands touching all significant areas, releasing one when you need to advance and grabbing hold of the next one.

Forward motion requires that you do more than simply throw items up in the air. You instinctively must know when to let go of ones that are no longer useful and to embrace those that can serve new, adaptive purposes. As one success leads to another, you will then be able to maintain your momentum and cover more ground, all without losing sight of your ultimate instinctive priorities.

Self-assessment exercise

How well are you currently juggling the various demands and responsibilities of your life? Are you moving forward or just barely keeping them up in the air? What steps do you need to take in order to advance forward?

_____

_____

_____

Memory challenge

Recall a time when you moved from one area of engagement to another. How did you handle the transition? What will you do differently the next time you make this leap?

_____

_____

Self-awareness exercise

Consider a time when you know you've dropped the ball and let something crash to the ground amid your juggling. What were the consequences of dropping this item? How did you recover?

_____

_____

Diversify Your Dreams

Sometimes you unwittingly limit yourself because you can't imagine juggling one more item in your day. You may falsely assume that all your endeavors require the same level of engagement, the same amount of time, or the same degree of involvement. But when you stop to think about it, you know that all the items you're juggling do not require the same level of exertion from you. While you may feel spread too thin, you may be expending more energy and investing more time in areas that are not productive or efficient with regard to your investment.

Instinctively juggling in the most productive ways requires you to look for overlapping opportunities and common denominators that can be combined. If your business model is instinctively designed, you will not need to develop a new one when you franchise your entrepreneurial endeavors.

Jugglers know how to delegate instinctively as well. When you find the right people for your team, then a crucial key to juggling successfully is utilizing them for maximum impact. Many others may be able to perform some of the tasks that you're juggling; these should be delegated so that you can concentrate on the areas that are instinctively unique to your fulfillment. All the more reason you want to surround yourself with instinctive individuals who move at your same speed. With similar rhythms, you can hand off items for them to juggle with little to no interruption.

Practical exercise

Review the list of responsibilities as well as priorities you made above. Flag the items you're currently juggling that are not squarely focused on your instinctive identity and advancement. Choose at least one item on your list to delegate—something you're currently doing that many others could do for you. Invest the time you gain into one of your key areas that needs more attention.

Self-awareness exercise

Identify an opportunity to enter a new area that you've delayed exploring because of all you're juggling. Make a list of common denominators this new field has with some of those you're already managing. How can this new ball fit into the mix of those you're already keeping in the air? Where does it overlap with other important areas of your life?

_____

_____

Application exercise

Look at your schedule for the next week. Cancel or postpone at least one unnecessary appointment, meeting, or event that's clearly outside your instinctive priorities. Use the added time to reconfigure your daily pace as well as to rest and renew your energy.

"The demands on your life don't have to be identical to be interrelated. That passion you have, the vibrancy of your intellect, the experiences you've garnered help propel you forward like a comet, grow into a planet, and soon become a new universe"

(*Instinct*, p. 231).

CHAPTER 19

✥

Your Instincts Adapt

Living instinctively requires constant adaptation to life's demands.

Technology changes so rapidly that it seems like you've barely gotten used to one new phone, laptop, or app before it becomes outdated. New software, new operating systems, and new hardware advancements make this constantly evolving field a fluid and dynamic network of ongoing changes. Living successfully by your instincts often requires just as much adaptation to change.

Memory challenge

When was the last time you felt unprepared for a sudden shift or change that was beyond your control? How did you respond to it? How have you prepared for another similar change or problem based on this experience?

_____

_____

No matter how successfully you're following your instincts, you will always need to adapt to the constantly changing world around you. Whether this requires daily tweaks or annual evaluations of your goals and methods, the actual execution will vary depending on your individual circumstances. However, change is the one constant that your instincts never ignore. Therefore, you must stay attuned to the evolution of the environment around you.

Some changes will be obvious and will have to be made in response to events and circumstances beyond your control. When the market shifts, when new competitors emerge, when new products launch, you know that you must take action. Even if you decide to take no action, that's still a decision you make deliberately and instinctively! Your own needs change over time along with the needs, goals, desires, and methods of the people around you. Living instinctively requires you to remain engaged with the present so that you can be prepared for the future.

Memory challenge

When was the last time you made a significant change or improvement in the way you do things? What precipitated this shift or change? What were the results of implementing this change?

_____

_____

_____

Self-assessment exercise

What's one constant in the way you typically approach fulfilling your responsibilities? Do you know what you need to function at maximum capacity? Better still, do you live according to what your instincts have revealed about the way you perform most effectively?

_____

_____

_____

_____

Your Instinctive Longevity

The example of the brontosaurus and its inability to adapt to change, discussed on page 237 in *Instinct*, provides a cautionary message for everyone. Unwilling to lower its neck to the foliage below its preferred tree-level nourishment, the brontosaurus apparently died because of its inability to adapt. Once its food supply diminished, it expired instead of adapting.

Similarly, you must also know when to make dramatic changes in order to survive. Whether this means relocating to another area, switching careers, investing what you've saved, spending an unexpected windfall, or forming new alliances, you must rely on your instincts or risk becoming extinct.

Just as your instincts can guide you in your daily deliberations, they can also assist you with your big decisions and life choices that have life-altering consequences. And perhaps more important, your instincts often serve as a bridge between your daily habits and your long-term goals. When you trust your instincts to guide you, connections between your daily details and your divine destiny will emerge before your very eyes. Like a beautiful mosaic, the small pieces of your life make up the masterpiece that will become your legacy.

Reflective exercise

How have your instincts shaped your long-term goals? How have your long-range instincts translated into daily habits? What corrective steps need to be taken in order to solidify the bridge between the details and the destiny, between today's needs and tomorrow's triumphs?

_____

_____

_____

Pensive points

What major life-changing decision is looming on the horizon for you? It may involve ending or beginning a significant relationship, starting a family, launching your own company, switching careers, going back to school, or retiring.

_____

_____

_____

What are you doing today to help yourself make this choice?

_____

_____

_____

Where do you see yourself a year from now? Five years from now? How can your instincts assist you right now in achieving this destination?

_____

_____

_____

Your Best Practices

One of the most powerful benefits of living instinctively emerges in your ability to make hard decisions in the face of change. This gift of discernment grows and ripens as the fruit of your activated instincts. When you have factual information and filter it through your instinctive sensibilities, you naturally become more adept at making important decisions.

Often these choices create lasting, even lifelong, benefits that in turn have a domino effect on so many other areas of your life. For instance, knowing the kind of lifestyle you ultimately desire often determines your spending habits today. You don't have to listen to your instincts to know that blowing your budget for a great pair of shoes today will sabotage the dream you have for starting an online shoe store in two years.

When operating at full throttle, your instincts can guide you toward what business gurus often call "best practices," the inherited wisdom of your predecessors applied to ongoing methods. Since you know that one size does not fit all in any situation or endeavor, then what works best for one person may not work at all for your own needs.

You may have to adapt what someone else did to fit your own unique situation. This reflects the beauty of your individuality and the divine creative gift of instincts to serve as your compass. You don't have to do things like everyone else; in fact, you must forge your own path in order to fulfill the specific destiny that is yours and yours alone.

Once you've developed systems and practices that work, you must remain vigilant to their effectiveness. While it's good and necessary to have strong default systems of operation in place, you don't want to miss opportunities because the ship of change sailed right past you. Establishing best practices must be tempered by remaining current with the changes and revised needs arising from evolving circumstances.

Setting any rule in stone can be dangerous if you're not willing to chisel a little deeper when things change! Today's best practices may be obsolete by next year. Your instincts will help you navigate the inherent tension between tradition and innovation, between your head and your heart, between what others want from you and what you want for yourself. You must never become so predictable or set in your ways that you end up being a dinosaur!

Self-assessment exercise

Which personal habits and preferred methods need to be reexamined in order to keep them current, effective, and instinctively attuned? Are there some that you already know need to be changed in some way? What has prevented you from adapting them already?

_____

_____

_____

Self quiz

Assuming you have the same roles and responsibilities that you're presently juggling, write out your ideal schedule for a typical workday.

☐ Would you rather sleep in and stay late?

☐ Go in early and leave after lunch?

☐ Work from home?

☐ Focus on one project or tackle several at once?

☐ Work alone or with a team?

☐ Think through the instinctive knowledge you've gained about yourself and how you work best. Be as specific as possible in scheduling the various requirements of your day.

_____

_____

_____

Practical exercise

Look at your ideal daily schedule and compare it to what you did yesterday. How do they compare? Where are they dramatically out of sync? What changes are within your power of control to make so that you can be more productive?

_____

_____

_____

"Relearning what you thought you knew well is important in every facet of life"

(*Instinct*, p. 240).

CHAPTER 20

✦

Your Treetop Instincts

*Instinctively focus on what's before you,
not on what's below you.*

As you instinctively ascend in your success, you will discover that there will almost always be others below you taking shots at you in flight. When I wrote op-ed pieces for a prestigious publication, I was initially dismayed at the virulent criticism each article seemed to generate for certain readers. It wasn't until I debriefed with the publication's editor, as I mentioned on pages 245–247 of *Instinct*, and then later on safari noticed giraffes eating from the tender leaves at the tops of trees, that I put two and two together to realize how important it is to remain focused on what's ahead and not what's behind, on what's above and not below. The higher you climb, the more people you may pass who will try to slow your ascent with unfounded criticism and jealous judgments.

Memory challenge

When have you been forced to contend with criticism that was unfounded, ill-informed, or simply directed (or misdirected) at you personally? How did you handle it at the time? How would you handle it now?

_____

_____

You must ignore these uninformed, destructive critics intent on impeding your progress for whatever personal reasons apparently motivate them—anger, jealousy, frustration, envy, or something else. You should always welcome constructive criticism, even when it's hard to hear. But the naysayers who belittle you for risking anew should never be taken seriously, and you should never give their stinging words the power to hold you back from your instinctive progress.

Reflective exercise

When was the last time you received constructive criticism that enabled you to improve your endeavors and methods? What's inherently different in this kind of feedback?

_____

_____

Self-awareness exercise

How have you allowed the criticism of others—whether destructively or constructively intended—to prevent you from attempting new challenges? How do you usually respond to your critics? In general, are you more likely to withdraw or to engage? To defend or to attack?

_____

_____

Your Treetop Appetite

If you want to continue to grow and to reach new heights of success, then you must learn from the long-necked giants of the bush. Giraffes instinctively know that the best source of nutrients for their unique physical needs comes from the food that happens to be at their eye level. They don't attempt to eat at ground level or chest level. As a result, they usually ignore those creatures clamoring around their feet. You must do the same.

As you instinctively ascend, you will require a different diet of information and relationships. Others might not understand your growth, let alone celebrate it with you. You must not stoop to their level. Don't undo your instinctive success because of others.

Self-assessment exercise

What are some of the changes you've made as you've become more successful in life? How have others responded to these changes? How have you handled the negative criticisms of those who clearly have hidden or personal agendas?

_____

_____

_____

Evaluation exercise

When have you lowered yourself and tried to respond to a critic's charges? Were you able to have a productive conversation? Or was it more of an emotional shouting match? What did you learn from this exchange?

Reflective exercise

When have you been tempted to criticize or belittle someone else's achievements or attempts at advancement? What was motivating your criticism? How do you usually handle ugly emotions—such as jealousy, resentment, and envy—when they emerge in response to the success of others?

_____

_____

_____

What's Feeding You

If you want to experience instinctive growth and fulfill your God-given potential, then you must replenish the sources that provide you with nourishment. Your body naturally knows that it needs fresh blood continuously coursing through it in order to replenish oxygen and nutrient supplies and to remove toxins. As you continue to explore and tame new territories, you will quickly realize that you must be a responsible steward of your increase and not merely a consumer enjoying a temporary fix.

Sustained growth requires your instinctive attention to the life-giving systems that fueled your successful ascent. You must replenish them consistently and regularly if you want to continue to climb to new heights of achievement. You don't want to reach a plateau—or worse, crash back to the ground where you started—because you neglected your own instinctive nourishment. Endurance athletes such as marathoners know they will crash if they don't remain hydrated and take in carbs for fuel. Similarly, you must also make sure you have the ongoing energy sources to sustain your journey.

Such replenishment also enables you to distinguish your adversaries from your allies more clearly. Those critics intent on your destruction will continually seek to sabotage the source of your instinctive power. Your allies, by contrast, will naturally collaborate with you to restore, revive, and renew the resources that feed the fire within you. When you feed what has fed you, then you're ensuring an ongoing source of nourishment for your future as well as for others coming along behind you.

Once again, you see that your instinctive wisdom is dynamic, adaptive, and creative. If you settle for status quo, if you view yourself as an entitled taker and constant consumer instead of a resourceful creator and caring contributor, then you miss out on enormous growth opportunities. And if you continue to deplete the resources that nourish your instincts, you will eventually discover that you've missed out on the most wonderful, satisfying soul food of all—the contentment of fulfilling your destiny.

Self-awareness exercise

Where have you been engaging beneath your abilities with critics who are only slowing you down? Where do you need to stop fighting and start flying?

_____

_____

_____

Interactive exercises

Write a letter to a specific person whose negative criticism has gotten under your skin. Address the specific points or mean-spirited language that upsets you the most. Tell them how you feel and conclude by letting them know that you forgive them and are moving on. From now on, you will no longer give them the power to slow down your instinctive progress. Decide whether you want to mail or e-mail your letter to this person, or whether to just keep it for your own cathartic awareness.

Write another letter to someone who has been an encourager, a cheerleader, a coach, and a sincere supporter of your instinctive advancement. Thank this person and let them know how they have made a difference in your life. Don't e-mail or text; write this letter the old-fashioned way, showing this person they're worth the time and attention it took to compose this letter by hand.

Practical exercise

Find an image of a giraffe online or in a magazine or other source. Print or cut out this image and post it in a visible place where you will see it each day—on your bathroom mirror, your car's dash, or your computer at work. Let it be a reminder to keep eating from the treetops and never to stoop to the level of any destructive detractors!

"If you want to live by instinct, feed your heart
and stretch to the treetops!"

(*Instinct*, p. 258).

CHAPTER 21

✦

You Have All That You Need

*You already possess the instinctive resources
you need to succeed.*

You have no idea how much vast treasure remains buried deep within you.
Thanks to the abundant and gracious bounty of your Creator, you have an
almost limitless supply of creativity, curiosity, and courage. Your instincts continue to unfold the vast treasure map to your soul's satisfaction as you explore
new possibilities and encounter unexpected opportunities.

Evaluation exercise

How have you noticed positive change since you started reading *Instinct* and working through the questions and exercises contained here? What's instinctively different about you now than when you began this process?

_____

_____

_____

Whether your instinctive excursion through life feels more like a safari or a pleasure cruise, an archaeological excavation or a mountain-climbing expedition, I hope you will continue on your journey with a greater awareness of all the resources within you. Through your instinctive, interior exploration in this application guide, I hope you feel more confident, more resourceful, and more equipped to enjoy the rest of your amazing journey.

I also hope that your instinctive appetite has been whetted to want more for yourself, to know instinctively that you can do anything necessary as you advance toward fulfilling what God has called you to do. Whether you feel the full confidence or not, you must believe that you have been given everything you need to take the next step toward your destiny.

Allow your faith to fuel a hope in accomplishing even more than you can imagine, knowing that God has brought you to this place and allowed your path to intersect with mine through the pages of *Instinct* and this application guide. He knows you have all you need within you, because he placed it there. You must trust in the knowledge of his goodness as you continue to allow the divine compass within you to guide your steps.

Reflective exercise

What three insights, tools, or new ideas will you carry with you from reading *Instinct* and completing these exercises?

_____

_____

What's been most helpful throughout this process of exploring your instincts and activating them within you?

_____

_____

You Have What It Takes

Confidence comes in many forms, and often you don't realize the personal resources at your disposal. This may be due to the fact that they've never been affirmed in you, or that you've never had to exercise them up until now. I'm convinced so much of what your instincts have to offer you is simply the faith to trust that you will survive and you will ultimately succeed.

Many days you wonder and can't even imagine how you will get out of bed and face the day. But you do! You muster up the courage, the grit, the divinely instinctive resolve within you and do the next thing that needs doing. You take one step and then another, and soon you have completed another mile along the journey.

You have already overcome so many obstacles to reach this moment, my friend. As you pause for a moment to catch your breath on your latest summit, do not look down and doubt yourself. Although you may still have many miles to go before you reach your ultimate goals, you have made it this far. You have not given up. You have pushed through discouragement, doubt, despair, and depression. You are a fighter, a survivor, and a masterpiece in the making! With instinct as your guide, you have only just begun to soar to new heights!

Self-awareness exercise

What obstacles have you overcome in the past year to get to where you are now? How have you persevered? What and who has sustained you? What role have your instincts played in this process?

_____

_____

_____

Memory challenge

Think back to a trial or difficult season in your life, a period when you weren't sure how you would keep going. What got you through that season? What did you learn about yourself from persevering? How has surviving and overcoming this time in your life become a source of courage and confidence?

_____

_____

_____

Self-assessment exercise

With these trials and obstacles you've overcome in mind, now list at least three of your attributes that helped you pass over these barriers. Don't be modest! How can you draw on these assets to instinctively advance even farther?

_____

_____

_____

You're Ready Right Now

If you've completed your reading of *Instinct*, and explored the inner you to discover your instinctive desires and abilities, then you are ready to make some bold moves! There's a reason you picked this book up in the first place. There's a reason you've pushed yourself and completed the soul searching and instinct-equipping effort through your experiences in this application guide. Even if you cannot yet identify what these bold moves might be, your instincts already know! You simply need to listen and to follow the voice whispering in your heart.

It may be time for you to take a risk of some kind. Don't lose your momentum now. Don't make any more excuses or allow any more obstacles to impede your instinctive progress. If you're attuned to your instincts, then you can sense the "urgency of now" I discussed earlier in *Instinct*.

You know it's true: your time is at hand. Don't delay. Use what you've discovered within yourself to move to the next level. It's time to leave the cage, fly out of the nest, and soar to new heights! I wish you Godspeed on the mighty adventure that awaits! You have all that you need to accomplish the mighty works for which you were designed!

Self-evaluation

Review what you've written and recorded in this application guide. What's been the most eye-opening discovery about yourself? How will you utilize what you've learned to live more instinctively going forward?

_____

_____

What chapters or passages have you returned to, reread, and underlined in both *Instinct* and this application guide? What's the most important message you've received from this experience?

_____

_____

Practical exercise

In the space below list three goals that you want to pursue in the next week as a result of how you've grown, changed, and become more instinctively aware. Begin at least one of them today. The time is now, so put your instincts in action!

_____

_____

_____

"You have what you need when you need it! Maybe not always exactly when you want *it—but when you* need *it"*

(*Instinct*, p. 260).

Appendix

Instinctive Animal Evaluation

As I share throughout *Instinct*, my safari in South Africa produced many powerful insights as I encountered various animals. Sometimes I think we may have more in common—at least instinctively—with these inhabitants of the wild than we realize. While it's just for fun, this questionnaire will help you discover which animal you most resemble in your instinctive inclinations.

Choose the response that best expresses your answer to each question or prompt. While more than one might apply, don't think too long about your response. Just go with your first instinct!

1. How do you most enjoy spending your weekends?
   a) relaxing at home with no schedule
   b) catching up on projects at work
   c) attending a new art exhibit
   d) planning your next vacation
   e) going out with friends spontaneously
   f) training for a marathon

2. Which of the following would you most enjoy watching?
   a) documentary on public television
   b) action-suspense movie
   c) independent film with subtitles

    d) motivational speaker on YouTube

    e) animated comedy or sitcom

    f) sports channel

3. You would describe the way you work as:

    a) slow and steady

    b) aggressively focused

    c) sporadic but productive

    d) always looking ahead

    e) collaborative and fun

    f) efficient and independent

4. How do you usually form impressions of others?

    a) several meetings or conversations over time

    b) how they compare to you

    c) their ability to pique your curiosity

    d) how they interact with a group

    e) their sense of humor

    f) their punctuality and ability to keep up

5. When making a presentation, what's your priority?

    a) giving yourself plenty of time

    b) using memorable visuals to make your points

    c) creating a dramatic attention getter

    d) focusing on the bottom line

    e) entertaining your audience throughout

    f) fast pacing that covers a lot of ground

6. Your ideal vacation would include:

    a) laying by the pool in a relaxed, sunny resort

    b) adventure-themed excursions with lots of activities

    c) boutique hotel in a large city overseas

    d) destination location with scheduled tour of sights

    e) tropical cruise with your closest friends

    f) large-group guided tour with a full schedule

7. Your family members would most likely describe you as:
   a) a careful planner who follows through on attaining goals
   b) a driven, focused competitor who knows how to win
   c) a quirky charmer who always surprises them
   d) a natural leader who's always looking ahead
   e) a fun-loving, integral part of the family
   f) a decisive quick thinker who's constantly on the go

8. How would you handle a conflict with your boss or supervisor?
   a) ignore the problem and keep going
   b) aggressively defend your position
   c) step back and take an unexpected approach
   d) focus his attention on the end result or shared goal
   e) diffuse the tension through humor
   f) reach a compromise or resolution as quickly as possible

9. Which of the following activities or events would be your least favorite?
   a) a fast-paced dance class
   b) a philosophical discussion on peace
   c) a weeklong conference with full schedule each day
   d) completing a list of small chores at home
   e) a silent personal retreat
   f) a leisurely drive with no real destination

10. Most days, your wardrobe would belong in the pages of:
   a) an L.L.Bean catalog
   b) *Vogue* or *GQ*
   c) *National Geographic*

    d) a Brooks Brothers catalog

    e) *Marie Claire* or *Esquire*

    f) *Runner's World*

11. When running late and stuck in traffic, you would probably:
    a) take a deep breath, relax, and turn up the radio
    b) take any available alternate route to keep moving
    c) drive across the median to create a shortcut
    d) use a phone app or computer to determine the length of the delay
    e) call your best friend to plan lunch next week
    f) call your office and delegate tasks until you arrive

12. Which of the following people do you most admire?
    a) Ronald Reagan
    b) Hillary Clinton
    c) Pablo Picasso
    d) Warren Buffett
    e) Tyler Perry
    f) Serena Williams

13. Imagine that you have to share some bad news with a close friend. Which sounds most like you?
    a) "Can we schedule some time together next week?"
    b) "I've got some bad news that you need to hear."
    c) "Remember the time when we had dinner at that little Italian place?"
    d) "I know it's hard, but look at the big picture."
    e) "Let's meet the gang for dinner and talk you through this."
    f) "Don't let this slow you down."

14. After receiving an unexpected promotion, you would celebrate by:
    a) increasing the withholding for your 401(k) or retirement account
    b) calling a team meeting to share your number one priority

    c) buying a new designer briefcase

    d) looking ahead at your next career move

    e) meeting coworkers for drinks after work

    f) moving into your new office space

15. You're most likely to trust your instincts when:
    a) planning for where you want to be in five years
    b) changing careers to start your own business
    c) redecorating your home
    d) writing the company mission statement
    e) cracking a joke during a meeting
    f) applying for a similar position with a competing company

16. If you could follow your natural pace each day, you would:
    a) take your time and complete one big task
    b) move slowly until motivated to expend a burst of energy
    c) jump from one thing to the next, finishing some, leaving others
    d) follow a schedule based on main priorities
    e) go with the flow and enjoy being spontaneous
    f) move rapidly to get as much done as possible

17. What's your favorite kind of social event?
    a) a relaxed, informal dinner party with six to eight people
    b) a formal fund-raiser with lots of movers and shakers
    c) an exclusive premiere party for a new play
    d) a professional luncheon with lots of networking
    e) a big theme party with dozens of people
    f) tailgating with various friends before the big game

18. How would you handle spilling coffee on yourself right before an important meeting?
    a) unruffled, you'd calmly clean up the spill as best you could

b) annoyed, you'd buy a new shirt to wear instead of the stained one

c) amused, you would ask for the brand name of the coffee

d) undisturbed, you'd change into a spare shirt you keep in your office

e) embarrassed, you would make a joke about it

f) agitated, you would rinse your shirt before anyone noticed

19. Which of the following characteristics annoys you the most in others?
    a) making hasty decisions before all the information is known
    b) having no real ambition or sense of direction
    c) conforming for the sake of fitting in
    d) focusing only on details and short-term solutions
    e) taking life too seriously
    f) moving slowly and indecisively

20. The kind of meal you would enjoy the most tends to be:
    a) an unrushed, home-cooked dinner with family and friends
    b) a catered dinner party in your honor
    c) a gourmet meal at your favorite specialty bistro
    d) a holiday gathering with everyone contributing
    e) an impromptu barbecue with friends who just dropped by
    f) a five-course meal that you've cooked yourself using new recipes

RESULTS

Now tally your results based on the number of times you selected each lettered response (a, b, c, d, e, or f). Which letter did you choose most frequently? Correlate the letter you chose most often with its safari animal. Do you agree with your type of animal? Or are you surprised? What kind of animal would you have selected prior to taking this little survey? Although this is imprecise and just for fun, it's sometimes quite revealing!

If you most frequently chose a), you're an ELEPHANT.

Slow and steady, elephants are planners who take their time and persevere to reach large goals over time. They're often no-nonsense, practical, solid, substantive, and determined. They don't like being rushed but can surprise others with how quickly they respond when circumstances require it. Elephants usually enjoy laid-back, relaxed environments with small groups of friends and family.

If you chose b) most often, then you're a LION.

The king of beasts is an aggressive hunter, always on the prowl and eager to chase its prey. Lions are driven, ambitious, and motivated by achievement and success. They take great pride in their appearance and exude a charismatic, dynamic quality that can sometimes intimidate others. They like being the center of attention but want to earn the respect and admiration of others for who they really are, not just their success.

If c) is your most frequent selection, you're probably a ZEBRA.

These unique, fun-loving creatures delight in being quirky innovators and creative catalysts. While their stripes may be black and white, zebras revel in shades of gray, comfortable with tension, compromise, and collaboration. They like original ideas and value taking risks to explore new possibilities. Often attracted to other zebras, they nonetheless enjoy mingling with the diverse menagerie of personality types they encounter.

GIRAFFES rise above your other options if you most often chose d).

A natural motivator who doesn't mind standing out in the crowd, giraffes keep their eyes on what's ahead and usually lead from the top down. They command respect for their natural abilities and unself-conscious ability to remain focused on the big picture. Giraffes never apologize for delegating the details to others below them. While traditional in many ways, these visionaries create lasting legacies by assembling a diverse team around shared goals.

If you chose e) more than other responses, then you might be a MONKEY.

Playful, spontaneous, and highly social, monkeys are creative communicators who bring a keen sense of humor and light approach to all endeavors. Rarely alone, their extroverted style and charismatic manner often appeal to many other types. Whether they're completing mundane tasks or innovating familiar systems, monkeys delight those around them with their funny stories, high energy, and clever ideas.

If letter f) expresses your responses most often, then you're likely a GAZELLE.

These graceful, quick-thinking, highly responsive types rarely stand still and are natural multitaskers. Gazelles use their speed to accomplish goals but may need to slow down to allow others to catch up and appreciate their trailblazing work. With an athletic intensity, these sleek masters of efficiency react well in a crisis, taking necessary actions immediately. Gazelles stay busy and tend to be incredibly productive in almost all areas.